Level Up Your Lesson Plans

Level Up Your Lesson Plans

Ignite the Joy of Learning with Fun and Educational Materials

TERESA KWANT

JB JOSSEY-BASS™

A Wiley Brand

Library of Congress Cataloging-in-Publication Data

Names: Kwant, Teresa, author.
Title: Level up your lesson plans : ignite the joy of learning with fun and
    educational materials / Teresa Kwant.
Description: Hoboken, New Jersey : Jossey-Bass, [2025] | Includes index.
Identifiers: LCCN 2025001252 (print) | LCCN 2025001253 (ebook) | ISBN
    9781394283507 (paperback) | ISBN 9781394283521 (adobe pdf) | ISBN
    9781394283514 (epub)
Subjects: LCSH: Lesson planning.
Classification: LCC LB1027.4 .K83 2025 (print) | LCC LB1027.4 (ebook) |
    DDC 371.3028--dc23/eng/20250204
LC record available at https://lccn.loc.gov/2025001252
LC ebook record available at https://lccn.loc.gov/2025001253

Cover Design: Wiley
Cover Image: © Africa Studio/stock.adobe.com
Author Photo: Courtesy of the author

SKY10101275_032725

To my best friend, who I am lucky to call my husband, this book is dedicated to you. From the very first cha-ching that brought in a whopping 30 cents, you believed in my potential long before I ever saw it myself. As my biggest fan, confidant, and inspiration, your belief in my creativity, strength, and determination—especially when I doubted myself—has meant the world to me. Thank you for being my greatest supporter, the best dad to our children, and the only teammate I would ever choose for this game of life and beyond. Love you!

Contents

Introduction

My professional journey began as a sixth-grade elementary teacher. While in the classroom, I discovered an online marketplace called Teachers Pay Teachers (TPT). Not only was I a teacher just finishing my third year of teaching, my husband and I had a new baby at home. After grading papers each night and putting our son to bed, I started exploring ways to make a little extra income. My initial goal was to be able to cover the grocery bill with a small side hustle. I didn't know how to create a product, start a business, or where to begin to sell a resource, but I dove right into the fire and gave it my best shot. It was messy. I made a lot of mistakes, but I saw some very big wins, too.

I vividly remember sitting in the teacher's lounge speaking with my coworkers who were also teaching sixth grade. I vaguely mentioned the TPT site and that I was possibly going to try selling something online. I had actually already started selling resources at this point but was scared to tell anyone. We joked around, and one teacher said, "You are going to be the next millionaire teacher." I laughed along with him, but in the back of my mind I thought, "Yes, I am. That's my goal." I was scared to admit this out loud, but not only was I going to replace my teaching salary, I was determined to far exceed it.

After five years in the classroom, and with a now toddler at home, I transitioned to a full-time teacher-author role, focusing on developing and selling classroom materials. The road to where I am today is quite unconventional for many teachers, but it is by no means unattainable. I still get the opportunity to impact classrooms, educate teachers on how to start their own businesses, and run a successful business of my own. My dedication to education remains, and I am excited to explore the benefits of my experiences with other educators. A supplemental income for teachers can be life changing. My objective is to empower educators and help them recognize their potential and value to generate passive income. I wholeheartedly believe in the expansive influence teachers can have, and it extends far beyond the confines of their own classrooms.

This book is all about mastering the art of lesson planning and crafting lessons that truly make a difference in the classroom. Exceptional lesson plans go beyond filling time or covering standards; they inspire, engage, and empower students to love learning. Throughout this journey, we'll uncover strategies to make your lesson plans effective, purposeful, and memorable, creating resources that help teachers and students alike.

Creating resources that impact student learning is no small task. It's a responsibility that requires thoughtful design, clear objectives, and a deep understanding of how lessons should flow. Slapping together a worksheet won't cut it. Effective resources require intention, clarity, and often an innovative twist that captures students' attention. That's why together we are going to explore the foundations of high-quality lesson planning. From setting up engaging hooks to structuring meaningful guided practice and assessments, we'll dive into ways to "Level up" your lesson plans in ways that students and teachers will love.

Here's the exciting part: At the final bonus level, we'll explore how you can take these lessons and turn them into an income stream that extends beyond your own classroom. Whether you need a little extra help planning thoughtful lessons or want to start a teacher side hustle, let's learn how to build confidence with intentional lesson planning, with the potential to reach more classrooms than you've ever imagined.

I fully believe school can and should be both educational and fun. In my experience, I have found that teachers are some of the most creative people in the world. They have to figure out, on a daily basis, how to teach multiple subjects to many different students, who all have different learning styles. This requires teachers to naturally be innovative, adapt easily, and solve a myriad of unexpected challenges that arise on a daily basis.

So, when you hear your class say "Are we doing anything fun today?" as a teacher, you probably begin to scream inside. On top of all the other responsibilities on your plate, you most likely want to exclaim, "Is this lesson not good enough for you?!"

However, I have some good news. Creating captivating and engaging lessons doesn't need to be complicated. There are six areas to making your lessons both compelling and enjoyable for your students that we will explore together (along with a few bonus levels to add to the fun). We'll examine each lesson plan component in detail. Think of this layout as your ultimate blueprint for crafting lesson plans. My goal is to guide you in adopting this model as you design your lessons, infusing them with content that is not only engaging and educational but also genuinely enjoyable. By following this framework, you'll be well-equipped to elevate your lesson plans, turning everyday learning into an exciting adventure for your students. And, who knows, maybe these lessons can also offer you a way to create a second stream of income. Let the games begin!

CHAPTER 1

Game On: The Level-Up Lesson Layout

I've always liked a good game plan. From knowing my entire life I was going to be a teacher to organizing lesson plans, or even planning a family vacation, watching everything fall into place gives me a sense of accomplishment. Having a game plan for my life is one way I find peace. So, when my first day as a sixth-grade teacher went off without a hitch, I expected most days to be the same. That was a young, naive, and very optimistic view. While I can look back on my teaching career with pride and remember most of my teaching days having well-thought-out game plans, the day I had my son was probably one of the worst-planned days of my life. In the end, things worked out, but we will cover that day in the classroom later.

I've always known I was made to be a teacher. This is evident from my earliest memories when I would boss my little sister around as we made makeshift classrooms for our dolls. I spent hours arranging my Barbies as students and dreaming of the time I could have real students of my own. Believe it or not, I even dreamed about correcting papers!

My journey as a teacher has evolved over the years. In college, I spent my time between classes at a local private school in its after-school program and then later as one of their preschool teachers. Every spare minute of my time was focused on learning to grow in a profession I was finally going to be a part of. As my university days came to a close, I spent my time as a student teacher in both second- and fifth-grade classrooms. This was a drastic turning point for me. While I first imagined teaching kindergarten or first grade, I soon realized upper elementary was where I wanted to be.

After graduating from the University of Utah with my bachelor's degree in elementary education, I was looking for a teaching position. It was summer, and I had my whole life ahead of me. For whatever reason, I thought it would also be a great idea to get my wisdom teeth out (want to keep those pearly whites straight!). So, as graduation ended and summer began, I headed to the oral surgeon to extract my wisdom teeth. Keep in mind, during this entire time, I was madly applying for any and all teaching positions I could find. I wanted to get hired closer to the beginning of the summer so I would have more time to plan and prep my classroom.

After the procedure, I headed home. A couple days later, I had an interview set up for an upper elementary teaching position. There were several positions open, so they were not assigning the grade levels until after the interviews. With a puffy face fresh from wisdom teeth removal, I walked confidently into the elementary school to meet the principal in my best skirt and blouse I could find, praying they lessened the distraction of my chipmunk cheeks.

I don't remember much about the interview other than loving the principal and instantly feeling a connection. She invited me to walk around the school, and I took that as a good sign that my puffy cheeks were not a problem. As she showed me the classrooms, the technology the school was equipped with, and all the building had to offer, call it intuition, but I knew I was going to work there. She hadn't offered me a job yet but had mentioned a sixth-grade teaching position that was open.

A few days later, I got the call. I was hired as a sixth-grade elementary school teacher. Just like I had hoped, it was near the beginning of the summer, and I would have plenty of time to plan, which would be necessary, because as I walked into room 123, I realized there was a lot of work to do. I found about six bottles of glue, a teacher's desk, and some student desks and chairs. That was it.

Luckily, I was given a grant as a new teacher, and with hundreds of dollars of my own money and some donations from my mom and mother-in-law, I got my classroom to where it needed to be to welcome new sixth-grade students. I prepared all summer, even taking the lesson plans and school books with me on vacations. Nervous doesn't even begin to describe how I felt, but I was going to be prepared. This is what I was made for.

I planned the first day of school down to the exact minute. I had getting to know you projects, team-building games, art lessons, and rule-setting activities so the first day would be fun for everyone. Setting up classroom rules and expectations were woven throughout that first day and first few weeks of school. I can't even count the hours I spent planning for that first day, but it paid off. I will never forget as the class was leaving, one boy happily smiling and shouting, "This was the best school day ever!" My goal was accomplished. I wanted students to not only learn in school but also *love* coming to school, too.

Sitting down at my desk after that first day of school, I felt happy, accomplished, and ready to tackle the world. While college can be a great introduction to teaching, it did not prepare me for what lay ahead: 30+ students, old school books, an expectation to teach subjects like science with little to no science materials, an assumption that I should write grants to get money to supply my classroom or use cash from my own pockets, and the realization that grading papers may not be as fun as I imagined when I was eight. However, I pushed on because I loved these kids, and I had a passion for education. This was where I was meant to be. My entire life led to this moment, and I was finally becoming the person I dreamed of being.

Fast-forward three years. Sometimes our lives don't go as planned. Sometimes, we have to go with the flow. And, sometimes, those spontaneous moments end up being the most memorable and happiest events of our lives. This is how I would describe the birth of my son. It was the middle of March, yet his due date was April 4th. I had my maternity sub plans fully put together at this point, but I was still madly writing updates to them and making sure all lessons were outlined correctly.

At the time, the school I was at was on a year-round schedule. This meant the classes were on different tracks, and our breaks were spread out throughout the year instead of being lumped together in one summer. We would usually teach nine weeks and then be off for two to three weeks. My son was supposed to be born during one of these breaks, and I was looking forward to saying goodbye for a time to my students and getting them all set up for when their substitute would return after their three-week break. My game plan was set to be a home run. My students were in capable hands while I was gone, plans were ready, and we were quickly approaching our time off.

One beautiful March morning, I woke up eager to finish out the school days ahead. We had just wrapped up parent-teacher conferences the week before, and I was exhausted. Assuming it was because of my pregnancy, I didn't think much of it. I had a checkup with my doctor the day before because I was feeling off, but nothing at the time seemed wrong. I squeezed my shoes on, which was a task because my feet were very swollen, and shuffled into school as only a pregnant teacher less than a month from her due date can do.

I taught almost the entire day. It was 2 p.m., and my students were at recess. I took a quick bathroom break and ran to the office, leaving my phone in the classroom. As I walked back through the office, the secretary stopped me and said, "Your doctor just called the school looking for you. She said you need to call her and get to the hospital immediately." I rushed to my classroom to find several missed calls from both my doctor and my husband. Apparently, this was an emergency if she was calling my school and husband!

While on the phone with my doctor, she informed me that some tests from the previous day came back and confirmed I had preeclampsia. I needed to get to the hospital immediately, and no, I could not wait to finish out the school day. This was an emergency. Suddenly, my plans were falling apart. We had three days until our break, I did not have those days planned for a substitute, and my students were counting on me. However, my health and the baby's health were at risk. So, I frantically left my students with my coworker and booked it to my car.

Upon reaching my vehicle, I discovered I had locked my keys in the car. Unbelievable. This was not the plan. Sheepishly, I made my way back into the office. After explaining my predicament to the office ladies and emphasizing the urgency of the situation, one of the secretaries took me to my house where I met my husband, and we then drove to the hospital. All the while, I am messaging a teacher friend, who was also my teaching mentor, asking her, while she is on her break, if she could come in and sub for a few days and explaining she may have to just wing it because I didn't have time in my hospital bed to make plans. This, may I add, is a strange responsibility teachers have and put on themselves. We feel the burden of educating these children no matter the scenario. We come to know our students on a level that no one else does for the year. We know all their challenges, successes, and setbacks. We know how best to suit their needs. Getting a sub even for a day can be overwhelming for a teacher, but for maternity leave? It's akin to the plans made for the Apollo moon landing.

Without going into much detail, since this isn't a book about pregnancy after all, 12 hours later our son entered the world. It was an experience I will never forget. At that moment, my greatest role as a teacher began: mother. This is a teaching position I have also always dreamed of achieving and one I do not take lightly. The role of a mother never ends and lasts through ages to come.

As you can see, over the years, my identity as an educator has evolved significantly. From beginning as a student myself and transitioning to a sixth-grade teacher to embracing the paramount role of motherhood (which I consider the most profound educational role I've ever undertaken) to teaching other teachers how to take their passion and turning it into a business, my love for teaching in any form remains undiminished. Creating engaging lesson plans doesn't need to be complicated and doesn't need to take a lot of effort. However, sometimes it does take some planning.

With this book, I hope to give you a game plan for leveling up your lesson plans and turn them into something both you and your students enjoy. I want to show you how to change ordinary days into extraordinary ones. Every lesson does not need to be a theatrical production. Each day does not need to be Instagram worthy. Your classroom does not need to look like it was plucked from Pinterest. However, having lessons that are engaging *and* fun can help you connect with your students, give learners a new way to achieve their learning goals, and can inspire your class to want to participate and grow.

So, let's begin! It's time to explore the power of *fun* in the classroom. I firmly believe school can and should be both fun and educational.

When students enjoy where they are and whom they are with, learning becomes second nature. It's time to introduce you to the roadmap of lesson planning I have created. We will dig deeper into each section as the book progresses, but let's take a peek at each of the elements.

"Leveling up" a lesson plan means enhancing and enriching your educational strategies to make learning more engaging, dynamic, and effective for students. We don't need to come up with a whole new structure for lesson planning, reinventing the wheel. What needs to happen is taking the bones of a good lesson plan and infusing it with teaching moments, connections with students, and activities that increase its potential to reach all learners in your classroom. So, drumroll please. Here is your blueprint to level up your lesson plans:

The Leveled-Up Lesson Layout:

1. Start Your Journey with Clear Learning Objectives
2. Press Play Using Engaging Hooks
3. Map Expansion: The Introduction of New Material
4. Join the Training Arena During Guided Practice
5. Multiplayer Mode Collaborative Practice in Your Lessons
6. Assessment: The Lesson Plan Victory Lap

CLEAR LEARNING OBJECTIVE

With every lesson, having a clear learning objective is essential for effective learning. It provides both the teacher and student with a specific learning goal. It helps a teacher know exactly what they need to teach and helps students know what is expected of them.

Learning objectives provide a purpose for the lesson and help students engage with the topic. Your students recognize the value in what they are learning, and why, when they see what the end goal is supposed to be.

Writing clear learning objectives also helps facilitate accurate assessment. The objectives provide criteria for which a student should be measured. This makes assessment more focused and meaningful.

Having clear learning objectives is like having a roadmap for teaching. They guide you in the right direction.

ENGAGING HOOK

A lesson hook can often make or break your lesson. An engaging hook is crucial because it serves to capture the attention of your students, and get them invested in what they will be learning. A well-planned hook can also pique students' interest in a subject they are unfamiliar with.

For example, science never came easy to me as a student or as a teacher. As a classroom teacher, science was a subject I had to study longer and research more because it was not a subject that I was confident in teaching.

However, one of my best lesson hooks each year came when I was teaching about the solar system. The lesson involved introducing my students to objects within our solar system, such as asteroids, meteors, and comets. The engaging lesson hook started with combining dry ice, water, dirt, dark corn syrup, and a dash of ammonia to create our own classroom comet! Students always loved this because learning about the solar system and planets is not tangible and often very abstract. This brought the solar system right into our classroom.

An engaging hook can set the tone for the entire lesson. It will get your students excited about the subject and interested in their own learning. With a good hook, you can engage all different levels of learners, while maintaining enthusiasm with all students.

INTRODUCTION OF NEW MATERIAL

The third building block for leveling up your lesson plan includes introducing the new material. This is the meat of the lesson where students encounter new material. After all, this is why we are at school: to learn and grow. Each day, students are filled with new information. Their brains are like sponges, soaking up the knowledge we give them.

Without learning, we would be stagnant with no progression. This is a critical point in the lesson.

This is the time in the lesson where new material challenges students' thinking and helps them develop higher cognitive skills like analyzing and evaluating what they are learning. These skills will help with their future endeavors as they develop problem-solving skills and learn to adapt to real-world situations. New material can also help reignite interest and motivation in students. Learning about different subjects and topics keeps the educational experience fresh and engaging. As teachers, it is our duty to keep that spark alive in our students' minds.

As a professional teacher, you are also aware that introducing new objectives and materials prepares students for more complex concepts in the future. This portion of the lesson, introducing the material, lays the foundation and skills necessary for understanding more sophisticated topics. When talking to teachers, you will often hear how they love to see those "lightbulb moments" where students are learning a concept and the information "just clicks." This happens by slowly building new material onto each other, one after another. It is an art that teachers master throughout their careers.

GUIDED PRACTICE

Once the objectives are outlined and the new material is taught, it is time for the next building block in leveling up your lesson plan, and that is the guided practice piece. I like to equate guided practice to when a teacher is student teaching. In college, you are introduced to the idea of becoming a teacher. Then, you get the opportunity to student-teach. The amount of time someone student-teaches varies, but in my experience, I student-taught for one year.

This was a huge turning point in my career. Since I was young, I always thought I would teach first or second grade or even kindergarten. While in college, I was one class away from getting my kindergarten endorsement when my professor placed me in a fifth-grade classroom to student-teach. She had watched me during other observations and lessons and had a hunch I may thrive more in a different classroom setting than what I had originally planned. I was shocked to find that I absolutely loved the older elementary kids. I enjoyed the curriculum and the personalities of the students. The reason for my shock wasn't that I didn't think I was capable of teaching older students, it was that my whole life plan was pointed in a slightly different direction, and one experience made an entire mind shift that I wasn't expecting. My professor saw something in me I hadn't recognized yet and guided me in a direction that, with her knowledge and teaching experience, helped her recognize where I could find success.

Without this guided practice before entering into my full-blown career, I could have made a huge mistake. While I believe I could have been a wonderful lower elementary teacher, my skills and personality were better suited for different ages. Guided practice for all students is critical because it allows the student to problem solve under the guidance of their teacher. The teacher can give feedback, answer questions, and support the student in crucial areas of their learning process to ensure the student learns and applies the skills necessary for success.

During the guided practice phase, learning is reinforced, immediate feedback is given, and confidence is built. This is also a time where students can actively engage in material, whether it is a game, activity, or practice problems, and apply concepts they were taught when material was introduced. Giving feedback is important because it helps students understand if they are applying their lessons correctly. Also, building confidence is necessary because it fosters a positive learning environment for students. When students feel safe, they can learn from their mistakes rather than having their mistakes tear them down.

COLLABORATIVE PRACTICE

The next building block for your lesson plan should be collaborative practice. In a world that is rapidly evolving and interconnected with technology, it can also feel extremely lonely. The importance of students learning to work collaboratively with others offers numerous benefits that are critical to personal, academic, and future professional goals. Collaborative practice should be included in as many lessons as possible. Students need this skill more than ever.

Growing up, I don't remember many instances of group or partner work. It was not a time when in education collaborative work was talked about. We sat in rows, and the room was expected to be quiet most of the time. However, times have changed, and teachers, thankfully, are beginning to learn that a classroom that is always quiet does not necessarily equate to students who are learning to the best of their ability. Collaborative work, in my opinion, is the most important piece of your lesson plan. This book will give you tools, ideas, and resources needed to successfully incorporate collaborative practice into your classroom.

Collaborative work helps students develop social skills like communication, conflict resolution, and empathy. As students work together, they learn to articulate their ideas, listen to others, negotiate their differences, and find solutions to problems. While technology is a great doorway to the world, it also isolates the people right in front of us. Students need to learn to interact in ways that don't include screens. Yes, collaborative practice can include technology, but we need to find ways to let students work together in a way that allows for active communication to take place.

Collaborative work also helps students build leadership skills. Group work encourages students to take on various roles within a team. This allows for practicing skills like decision-making, accountability, and delegation. Learning to manage a piece of a project or lead a team will be valuable assets that serve students beyond a classroom.

Students can also learn to be flexible as they work in a group. Situations can change, and expectations may adjust. Our world is filled with change, and learning to accept change is a skill students can practice while working on collaborative projects or activities in the classroom.

ASSESSMENT

The last building block in your leveled-up lesson plan should be assessment. Assessment is important because it provides feedback about the learning process for both teachers and students. Figuring out what students understand from your teaching is a critical piece of education. Assessment will guide instruction and is instrumental in setting learning goals for students to progress through the school year.

In your leveled-up lesson plan, the assessment will most often be formative rather than summative. Formative assessment is done while the learning is taking place, and summative assessment is used to evaluate student learning at the end of an instructional unit. Formative assessment often works best for individual lessons.

Some formative examples of assessment that you could use to level up your lessons include the following:

- **Think-pair-share**: As you are teaching concepts, ask students to think about a question individually. Then, allow them a minute or two to discuss their thoughts with a partner. Finally, students will share conclusions with the class. This method allows the teacher to quickly assess students' understanding.
- **Exit tickets**: At the end of class, students fill out a small card, or half slip of paper, and answer a few questions from the lesson. They can even add something they found interesting or confusing from the day. This will help teachers gauge what students need help with on the next lesson.
- **Polls or quizzes**: These can be done with paper and pencil or with classroom clickers for online responses. Offering feedback, polls, and quizzes can guide a teacher into what the next steps in instruction should be.
- **Two stars and a wish**: With this formative assessment, students list two things they feel they understood well from the lesson and one concept they wish they knew better or found confusing. Using this assessment helps students reflect on their own learning.

With the building blocks of a good lesson plan set, it is time to start leveling up your own lesson plans. In the following chapters, we will discuss ways to add engagement, fun, and collaboration to each section of this lesson layout. Also, you will find lesson ideas that you can bring straight into your classroom. As Mark Van Doren said, "The art of teaching is the art of assisting discovery." I hope to assist you in discovering the best ways to level up your lesson plans and create a classroom space that fosters learning in the best ways possible. Make sure to use the template provided (see Figure 1.1) as you move through the book and write your lessons!

Leveled-Up Lesson Plan

Subject:

Date:

Grade Level:

Clear Learning Objective	Engaging Hook

Introduction of New Material	Collaborative Practice

Guided Practice	Assessment

Materials Needed	Notes

FIGURE 1.1 Leveled-Up Lesson Plan template

To access all the bonus material for this book, simply scan this QR code or type the URL in your browser.

teresakwant.com/bonus-material/
Password: levelup

CHAPTER 2

Start Your Journey with Clear Learning Objectives

I clearly remember my first year teaching and going to a faculty meeting titled "SWBAT." As a teacher fresh out of college, I was not yet fluent in the secret code of acronyms that teachers conjure up. But I would quickly learn, as all newbie teachers do, educational acronyms are the way of the teacher world.

In the faculty meeting, I learned that SWBAT stood for, "Students will be able to. . .," and I was to use it when writing objectives on the board during each lesson. For example, "Students will be able to multiply a four-digit whole number by a one-digit whole number." Now, I am not here to debate whether having objectives written on your board will magically make all your students proficient in the objective being taught. However, I do think it is important to have objectives for each lesson and to inform your students what those objectives are.

Having a clear objective for your lesson is like having a roadmap for a vacation. It helps guide you in the correct direction, and you can refer to it to ensure you made it to your final destination. Objectives also help students stay focused on their learning. They lead not only the teacher but the students where they need to go.

When writing a lesson plan, you must always start with the objective. The objective will be the focus of the entire lesson. Sometimes, an objective may span multiple lessons, but it should always be at the center of what you are teaching. Objectives bring purpose to learning. In fact, they provide a pivotal role in the educational process because they set clear, focused, and achievable goals for both educators and students. These objectives also play a role in the direction the teacher will take when teaching content. Objectives should be in sequential order and build on each other.

From a student's perspective, learning objectives make education understandable and relatable. They have a goal to shoot for. Students have a plan and know what to focus on when learning. Your students are more likely to engage with topics when they know what the material is they are learning and why they are learning it. Clear objectives can also help students self-assess their progress and identify areas they need to concentrate their efforts more on or seek additional help.

As you write your objectives, keep the SMART acronym (see, teachers just love these things!) in mind. It will help you remember the characteristics of an effective objective.

S – Specific: Clearly define your goal for the lesson.

M – Measurable: Objectives should allow for assessment of student progress.

A – Achievable: Make the objective realistic and attainable for students' learning levels.

R – Relevant: Always connect the objective to a specific standard.

T – Time-bound: Allow for each objective to be taught within a specific time frame.

One way to make sure you are being specific with your objective is to use clear action verbs. The strong action verbs should provide an unambiguous communication of what students are expected to do. For example, verbs like *analyze, demonstrate, create,* and *compare* all spell out the action students will do while learning the objective.

You can also set specific criteria for what the mastery of the objective looks like. If the standard is to "compare two 2-digit numbers based on meanings of the 10s and 1s digits using the symbols <, >, and = ", you might add criteria like "by solving comparison question cards in class." Objectives that start with strong action verbs are inherently more measurable. When you use verbs like *illustrate* or *analyze*, you can directly observe if the students are performing these actions. Vague verbs like *learn* can be subject to interpretation. They do not offer an easily measurable goal because they are nonspecific and challenging to assess directly.

Make sure you are familiar with the standards you need to teach your students for your subjects and grade levels. Before the lesson planning process even begins, you should have spent time mapping out the objectives and standards for the entire year. Which standards will you teach first and in what order? This planning phase, although time-consuming, is a vital investment. Deciding the sequence in which to teach the standards will help structure the year's curriculum logically. To help with the process, I have provided curriculum pacing guides in Chapter 11 of this book!

As you draft your yearly plan, consider how the different standards across different subjects interconnect and support each other. Use tools by your state or district departments to help write these detailed plans. Keep in mind that while these plans are essential, maintaining flexibility while teaching is also necessary as student's needs are dynamic and learning opportunities evolve throughout the year.

Making sure the objective is achievable for students is necessary not only for their educational experience but also for their confidence in school as well. As you write your objectives, remember that less is more. For a fourth-grade writing standard like "Introduce a topic or text clearly. State an opinion, and create an organizational structure in which related ideas are grouped to support the writer's purpose," you may consider breaking this down into two to three objectives as you introduce the standard. The first part might be "Students will be able to introduce a topic or text clearly in their opening paragraph of their opinion essay." Your next objective might be "Students will be able to state an opinion, while giving facts and examples to support their reasoning, throughout their writing." Breaking down the standards makes it less overwhelming for students and easier for them to grasp the concept. They won't feel rushed and can find small successes that build on each other, until they eventually master the entire standard.

Next, you should have goals for when you want the standards you are teaching to be mastered. First, understand your student's capabilities. Knowing where your student's current knowledge stands, by using assessment data, will be a guiding factor in developing how long it should take to grasp each objective being taught. Most objectives, because they are smaller portions of a standard, should take one lesson, maybe a couple more, to master for most students. However, keep in mind what is required for the unit as a whole; one lesson is just the stepping stone for more to come. You want to ensure learning is thorough but not rushed.

Before we dive into ways to make introducing objectives fun to your students and leveling up your objectives in your lesson plans, let's take a quick look at some well-written objectives:

Fourth Grade: Literacy.RI.4.2, Determine the main idea of a text and explain how it is supported by key details; summarize the text.

Objective 1: Students will be able to identify the main idea of a given paragraph by selecting the correct statement from a list of options.

Objective 2: Students will summarize a one-page text in three to five sentences, accurately conveying the text's main idea and essential details.

Objective 3: Students will demonstrate the ability to explain how key details support the main idea of a text by writing three supporting sentences in their own words.

Objective 4: Students will differentiate between main ideas and supporting details in a mixed list and correctly categorize at least five given statements.

As you can see, there was one standard, which on the outside looked quite simple and straightforward. However, we were able to create four different learning objectives. You will notice there are strong verbs like *identify, summarize, demonstrate*, and *differentiate* to help the teacher and student recognize what needs to be accomplished. Each objective also outlines how the objective will be met, like in objective 1 when it says, "By selecting the correct statement from a list of options." These standards are clear, have strong action verbs, and lay out how the learning will be assessed.

Once you have your objective(s) for your lesson written, it is time to level it up! You can just post the standard as an "I can statement" on the board. "I can identify the main idea of a given paragraph by selecting the correct statement from a list of options." However, that isn't fun! And to be honest, the students may not even look at the objective that often. Yes, put the objective on the board, but let's explore ways for students to *want* to know what the objectives are for their lessons and ways to help them be an active participant in their learning.

Let's compare two different classrooms. In a fourth-grade classroom, Mrs. Miller starts her reading lesson as usual by writing the objective clearly on the board. In bold letters she writes, "I can determine the main idea of a text and explain how it is supported by key details." Mrs. Miller doesn't spend much time explaining what a main idea is or even offering an explanation for the term *key details*. She assumes the objective is clear enough. After all, she wrote it on the board.

As the lesson begins, Mrs. Miller instructs the students to take out their reading books. She then begins to read aloud a selection of the text. Occasionally, she pauses and points out a main idea and the supporting details; however, the conversation is often one-sided, with several students staring into the abyss. Some students seem to be listening but are doing so passively. Others are attentive but not quite sure what they are to be doing, and why.

After the reading, Mrs. Miller instructs the students to write down the main idea and some key details of the story in their notebooks. As Mrs. Miller walks around the room and offers assistance, the energy among students is low. The students seem to complete the task as they are instructed; however, there is little enthusiasm or deep engagement. The learning objective may be clear, but it is static and presented in a traditional format that may not resonate with all learning styles. The objective remains just a statement on the board that students should be able to do, but not something they feel actively involved in achieving.

Let's contrast this with Mr. Lee's class. As his lesson begins, Mr. Lee holds up a file that has "Top Secret" in bold, red letters written on the front of the folder. He tells the class they are detectives on a special reading mission. Mr. Lee explains that inside the top-secret file is a mysterious manuscript that holds the answer to the keys they need to discover.

At this point, the entire class is intrigued and interested in what Mr. Lee is presenting. "What secret mission are they about to embark on?" the students wonder.

Mr. Lee (quite dramatically, might I add) peers into the folder and announces, "There is an objective!" He then reads the secret mission to the class, "Students will be able to read the top-secret manuscript and identify the text's main idea and three supporting key details in a written paragraph." Mr. Lee goes on to write this objective on the board and explains that the secret manuscript, also within the file, holds the answers to what they are looking for. The manuscript is the text they will be reading and exploring together. The students are excited for their learning adventure.

As Mr. Lee passes out the text found in the secret file to his students, he tells them they are reading detectives ready to solve today's myste-rious Main Topic reading mission. At this point, students are thrilled to be learning because they are not just students but detectives. They are actively participating in their learning. The students read the text together, debating among themselves what the main topic and details of the text are.

After the readings, student groups are asked to present their case to the class. They are to explain their reasoning for finding the main idea of the text as well as its supporting details. Groups took turns explain-ing their findings and expressing their thoughts. The detectives take their work very seriously!

At the end of the lesson, Mr. Lee congratulates his class on complet-ing their mission. He looks back on the standard written on the board and clarifies how the secret mission was a success. Mr. Lee congratu-lated his class on a job well done and told them they were able to cor-rectly identify the main topic and details of a text. The class was actively engaged in the learning process.

Both of these stories illustrate a teacher introducing an objective to the class. Both options were very simple and took little preparation. However, with Mr. Lee, his students were intrigued by the mystery and were excited to be "Detectives." The way in which Mr. Lee presented the objective allowed for students to be interested in what they were learning and more willing to give the lesson a try. They weren't just reading a text; they were reading a top secret manuscript!

When writing a Leveled Up Lesson Plan, consider introducing your objective for the lesson in a fun way like Mr. Lee. The introduction of the objective does not require a lot of effort. However, with some creative thinking, you can definitely make it a memorable learning experience for your students.

LEVELED-UP LEARNING OBJECTIVE IDEAS

It's time to explore ways you can introduce the objective for a lesson to your students. Remember, introducing an objective does not (and often, probably shouldn't) be extravagant. The key is to get your students interested in what they are learning. Here are some strategies for introducing learning objectives in ways that are both effective and engaging:

- **Mystery box**: Create a box that can be placed at the front of your classroom. Decorate it, paint it, make it as pretty as you would like! Label it "Mystery Box." Each day, place the objectives for your lessons inside. At the start of each lesson, have a student read what the mystery learning objective is for the lesson. The suspense of what is inside will capture the attention of your students. Make it a little more interesting by adding an object. Students will need to determine how the object relates to the objective.
- **Objective quest cards**: This is a simple idea that can be used for the entire year. At the beginning of each unit, create cards for each objective. Students can collect the cards as the lesson is completed or as they master each objective taught. Then, students can save the cards on a ring to show their friends and family. Or, the cards could be used as classroom money. At the end of the year, students can use their objective quest cards for a drawing or to buy from a class store.
- **Crack the code**: Create a simple code for the letters of the alphabet. For example, $A = 1$, $B = 2$, $C = 3$. Write the objective using the code. Have students decipher their learning objective for the lesson.

- **Objective karaoke**: If you are musical (I am not, but I find a lot of talented teachers on YouTube), turn the objective into lyrics to a current popular song. This will help the students remember what they are learning in a unique and interesting way!
- **Odd one out**: Write four different statements on the board. One will not fit among the group. The odd one out will be the objective for the day. This will get students reasoning and thinking together. While simple, this method does allow for critical thinking and gives students an opportunity to think outside the box.
- **Image slideshow**: Show some images that relate to your objective. Allow students to work with a partner and come up with vocabulary words for each image. Then share the vocabulary words with the class. Using as many of the words students created from the images as you can, write the learning objective for the lesson.
- **Objective relay**: Start by dividing your class into teams. Before the game starts, write the objective on the board with zero explanation. Give the teams time to discuss what they think the objective means. Then, line the teams up. Allow one member from each team to race to the board at a time. They are to write what they think the objective means. Before allowing the next students to race to the board, identify which team was the closest to the meaning. When the objective is clear, begin the lesson.
- **Illustrate it**: Start by writing the objective on the board. Then pass out a blank card to each student. As you discuss what the objective means and the goal for the day, have students illustrate what they think the objective means. At the end of the lesson, allow students to revise their drawings as needed.
- **All mixed up**: Write the words of the objective on the board, but write them out of order and all mixed up! Let students work with a partner and try to put the words in the correct order for the objective. Allow partner groups to share their answers.
- **Graphic organizers**: Use a graphic organizer, like a KWL chart to help students understand what they will be learning. Begin by writing the objective on the board. Ask students what they already **K**now about this subject. Have them write it in the **K** section of their chart. Then ask them what they **W**ant to know about this subject.

Instruct them to write it in the **W** section of their chart. Finally, when the lesson is over, review the objective again and ask students what they Learned. Have them put their answers in the **L** section of their chart.

You didn't know learning objectives could be so fun, did you? Think of your "students will be able to" (SWBAT) standards not just as items on the board but as the starting line of an educational race. Every day, you're the game master, unveiling the quest of the day to your eager team of learners.

Ultimately, the end prize of the game of learning is autonomy or the ability for the student to take charge of their learning. As educators, we are the guides of this journey. We craft and create the lessons, from the objective down to the assessment, with the hope of a greater understanding that eventually leads the students to independence.

So, the next time you write down your learning objective for a lesson, remind yourself you are not just teaching students; you are igniting the spark of exploration. Every lesson is one more level mastered in the game of school!

CHAPTER **3**

Press Play Using Engaging Hooks

Several years ago, I noticed a product in my online shop was getting more attention than normal. When I checked where the traffic was coming from, I noticed it was YouTube. This was odd since, at the time, I did not have a YouTube channel. I could not figure out where on YouTube this traffic was coming from. At the time, my son was six, my oldest daughter was three, and my newest baby daughter was only a couple of months old. Creating videos was out of the question. So, who had created a video and led people to my online store?

The mystery continued for several days. In between finding precious moments to nap (something hard to do with a newborn) and trying to keep my business afloat, I came across a YouTube account of a teacher. As I scrolled through her videos, I noticed a video of the teacher dressed as a pirate and explaining her pirate-themed day with her students to her audience. I was enamored! What a great way to get your students excited to learn. This teacher made an impression on me from the second I saw her video, so I continued watching. She explained how she was going to read a pirate book with her student's and then do an escape room that was pirate themed to review content from the year.

Imagine my utter shock when this teacher held up the game she was going to do with her students, and it was one of *my* escape rooms I had created! I could not believe it. This teacher's YouTube channel had hundreds of thousands of followers. I felt like I had just won the lottery. Here I was, holed up at home with two young kids plus a baby, dreaming of making an impact with students again but not knowing if my efforts behind a computer screen were paying off, only to come across just one example of a teacher using one of my escape rooms for her students and sharing the experience with her extremely large audience of teachers all over the world. I was humbled to say the least. At a time in my life where I was unable to be in a classroom, I was still able to help make an impact on the lives of teachers and students. It was an incredible feeling.

This teacher went above and beyond the call of duty as she prepared her pirate-themed day. She was reviewing math skills and decided to use my pirate math review game. Her hook was to get the students excited about learning by dressing as a pirate for the day and reading some pirate stories. While a hook for your lesson doesn't need to always be this extravagant, every once in a while it does add a bit of fun to your teaching.

Writing a hook for a lesson plan plays a critical role in your teaching. In education, a "hook" refers to an engaging strategy used at the beginning of the lesson to capture the student's attention and get them excited about the topic being taught. It serves as the entry point that draws students into the learning. A good hook will stimulate interest in the students. While a hook can take various forms like anecdotes, questions, visuals, activities, slide shows, and presentations, the key similarity for all hooks is that it motivates learners right from the start.

Why are hooks an important piece of any lesson plan? First, they capture the attention of the students. Students today are bombarded with distractions. They are constantly pulled in different directions. By starting a lesson with a well-thought-out hook, you can teach students to rein in their attention to what is being taught.

Second, a good hook also creates relevance for the lesson. When you create a lesson hook that relates to your student's interests, current events, or even pop culture, you instantly create an atmosphere that is relatable and a lesson that is meaningful in the eyes of your class. Not only will a good hook create relevance, it will also help build classroom community.

There are many different types of hooks you can use in your lessons. For example, you could begin with a thought-provoking question that stimulates curiosity. While it might be easy to state a question at the beginning of each lesson like "Have you ever heard the word *sway* before?" and then begin a persuasive writing lesson, there are more creative ways to hook your students that are just as easy. In fact, I find asking questions the easy way out when it comes to writing a hook for a lesson. While they have their place occasionally, it's time to branch out and try some new strategies. I will not leave you hanging! It's time to go over a few different hook strategies.

- **Personal engagement**
  - *Purpose*: This type of hook would mean using personal anecdotes or stories to gain the attention of your students. This type of hook creates a connection between the teacher and students and humanizes the topic. Students are likely to remember information when presented in a personal context that resonates with their own experiences.
  - *Example*: "Today we are going to be talking about resilience. Before I explain what that word means, I want to share a story about a time I was in high school. I was a sophomore cheerleader and wanted to try out for the varsity squad. This was a big challenge because many of the sophomore cheerleaders move up to the JV team before they advance to the varsity team. It took a lot of practice and effort to learn the routines and cheers for the tryouts. On the day of the tryouts, I was very nervous; however, I gave it my best shot. I did my routines, tumbling and cheers to the best of my ability. The night the varsity cheer team was announced, there was a big party at the school in the gym. Everyone gathered to hear who made not only the cheer team but also the basketball team as well. To my disappointment, I did not make the varsity cheer team that year. However, this experience taught me an important lesson: resilience. I learned to bounce back and not give up. I ended up trying out for the JV cheer squad instead. Not only did I make the team, I became team captain. This experience taught me that sometimes life doesn't go as we plan, but things can still work out. This event in my life didn't just teach me about working hard, it taught me how to overcome obstacles, and it reminded me that setbacks are part of the journey in life. How we respond to these setbacks shapes our growth and success."

- *Explanation*: With this hook, the teacher instantly connected with their students by sharing a personal setback from their own life. By recounting their experience of resilience and eventual success, the teacher not only demonstrated the concept of resilience in action but also encouraged students to see setbacks as opportunities for growth. This personal story humanized the lesson on resilience and helped the students relate to the concept and apply it in their own lives. Now the students can feel connected and look for ways in their lives they can turn setbacks into triumphs. This simple hook lured the students in and made them invested to learn about resilience.

- **Visual hooks**

  - *Purpose*: With a visual hook, you are appealing to students' who have visual learning preferences. In today's world, kids are constantly surrounded with screens and visualization. Photos, videos, or any visual representation can provide a concrete representation of complex ideas or abstract concepts.

  - *Example*: As students walk into the classroom, have different photos of the Milky Way projected on a screen. "In science, we will be exploring outer space. This is a topic we will be focusing on for several weeks. On the screen are several photos of the Milky Way. I want you to take out your science journals and imagine you are an astronaut zooming through space. What adventures will you go on? Picture yourself cruising by planets, gazing at stars, and exploring the galaxy. What topics do you hope to study in our outer space unit? Write those ideas down, and we will share them when we are done examining the photos and writing our journal entries."

  - *Explanation*: As students enter the classroom, the first thing they see are the pictures of the Milky Way. These photos pique their interest, and they begin to wonder what they will be learning about. Since space is less concrete for students and something they aren't dealing with on a daily basis, bringing photos in creates visuals and brings the topic to life. The photos stimulate their imagination and lays a foundation for what is to come. This hook helps the lesson be memorable for the students. The teacher can now segue into their outer space unit, and students have a visual in mind of what is being discussed.

- **Interactive hooks**
  - *Purpose*: This type of hook aims to engage students through interactive play or hands-on activities. With interactive hooks, you are requiring students to actively participate right from the beginning of the lesson. By involving students right from the get-go, you are setting the tone for collaboration and deeper exploration of lesson content.
  - *Example*: "We are beginning our study of *Sherlock Holmes*, by Sir Arthur Conan Doyle. Sherlock is a detective who solves mysteries. Before we begin, I have a small mystery reader's theater. Each of you will have a part, and we will read the mystery together, voicing our own parts. After we have read through our reader's theater one time, we will try going through it again while acting out our different parts. When finished, we will begin our reading of *Sherlock Holmes* and find comparisons between the reader's theater and the *Sherlock Holmes* mystery."
  - *Explanation*: This is a great introduction hook for a unit of mysteries involving Sherlock Holmes because right from the beginning students are immersed into reading, acting, and feeling what a character in a mystery would be like. Students are encouraged to think critically and find comparisons from the reader's theater and then the actual story of Sherlock Holmes they will be reading together as a class. This example opens students up to one type of mystery in the reader's theater before introducing them to the main reading for the lesson.
- **Theme-based hooks**
  - *Purpose*: Theme-based hooks create a cohesive and memorable learning experience. While they do often take more work, if well planned, these types of lesson engagers can set a vibrant and engaging tone for your students. Themes can also be spread out through multiple lessons making them great for incorporating other subject areas. With a theme-based hook, it could involve

dressing up, creating a themed environment, or incorporating thematic elements throughout the lesson.

- *Example*: Arrive in class dressed like a paleontologist. Wear a hat, cargo pants, vest, and boots, while carrying binoculars, a compass, a magnifying glass, and a notebook. Consider decorating your class with some dinosaur cutouts and palm trees. "Welcome to Jurassic Math Park! Today we will be stepping back in time to explore math through the eyes of paleontologists. We will measure dinosaur footprints, solve math puzzles based on fossil discoveries, calculate the sizes of different dinosaur species, and collect data on different food that dinosaurs ate. Get ready to jump back in time and explore math through the eyes of a paleontologist."

- *Explanation*: This hook would require preparation and planning; however, it is a lesson students would never forget! In fact, I bet your most reluctant learners would enjoy learning math in the Jurassic Park! Since this type of hook does require more planning, I would encourage teachers to incorporate their other lessons throughout the day into the theme. Make it a whole dinosaur and paleontologist day (or whatever theme you choose). For example, read books about dinosaurs, do some science experiments with fossils, and create art projects where students create their very own dinosaur! The idea of this hook is really to help your students step into the lesson and be immersed in the content and theme. These types of hooks and lessons are great for big themed days, or scattered throughout the year, but do not feel pressure to make every lesson each day this thematic. That would burn any teacher out!

I would like to share a hook from a lesson that had an impact on me as a student growing up. Going to middle school is an interesting experience. It's that complex, yet often defining moment, in a child's life where everything seems to change at once. One day, they are in elementary school with a teacher guiding them through each step and lesson they learn, the next they are forced into crowded halls, attending multiple classes, and carrying a bag full of homework weighing them down, to complete for the week.

Middle school may not be everyone's highlight reel of school memories; awkward doesn't even begin to describe those years! However, amid all the cringeworthy moments, I did have a geography teacher who left an incredible impact on my life. Her name was Mrs. Parker. At my middle school, all ninth graders were required to draw an entire map of the world by the end of the year, strictly from memory. It had to be spot on. No borders left undrawn! Each student would draw the entire world in one sitting in their World Geography class. This class was like a rite of passage for kids at my school. It was the pinnacle moment of each student's ninth grade year. Here's the kicker: it wasn't just about geography. In the end, this class taught us life lessons that stuck. First, we learned that persistence paid off. Second, it proved that even the toughest tasks get easier with practice. Lastly, and most important, we learned that progress was more important than perfection because while we had to have borders correct for each country, it did not need to be perfect. We just needed to show where one country ended and the next began. In the end, Mrs. Parker's class was more than just learning about the world—it was about learning perseverance and understanding that sometimes the journey matters more than the destination.

One day, about midway through the year, Mrs. Parker told us we were going to start learning about the countries of Africa. She began by saying this would be the hardest continent to draw because it had the most countries, but she had a trick to help us make it one of the easiest parts of the world map to draw; a song! If my memory serves me well, she then pulled out a cassette tape, not even a CD, to begin playing a song that named each country in Africa. Spotfiy was nonexistent in the early 2000s. In fact, I wouldn't be surprised if students in my class tried downloading the Africa song from Napster to study their map drawing. What made this song great for when we were learning to draw the continent of Africa was that it named each country from north to south, in order. While this song was to hook us into learning about Africa, it eventually became the cornerstone for learning the continent's countries in order.

Speaking of hooks, Mrs. Parker made the hook of her introduction to Africa lesson relatableby stating she was going to make the hardest part of our test one of the easiest. All the students could breathe a sigh of relief in knowing they could have one of the toughest continents memorized for the final. Mrs. Parker then lured us in by playing a song that would eventually be a necessity for our test. Next, our brilliant teacher activated our curiosity by suggesting we learn and memorize the song together. We eventually sang this song on a daily basis to help us study for the test. Last, Mrs. Parker yielded to creativity and made learning fun. She made the hook of her lesson about Africa memorable, so memorable, might I add, that 25 plus years later I can still sing the continents of Africa today!

Talking with family and friends who went to my school and took this class, we have all mentioned how it has impacted our lives and stuck with us. The simplest hook, a song about Africa, has stuck with hundreds, if not thousands, of students today. And it was not only the song but the task of drawing the map itself. Ask me about any country in the world, and if I don't know exactly where it is anymore, I can at least give you a general idea. I will also never forget where Lebanon or Luxembourg are on a map, which were the two countries I forgot to label on my test.

Now that we have a general idea of what a lesson hook is and the importance it can have on your lesson to set the tone for the learning, I have a tool to help you craft the perfect hooks for your lessons! Don't worry; I haven't forgotten the love of acronyms teachers share, so I have devised a handy acronym to guide you in creating hooks that aren't just relatable but also irresistibly engaging and fun. It's time to press Play and spark curiosity from the moment students walk into your classroom. Once you have set your objective and launched your hook, your lesson is in motion. It is imperative you get it right. It's game time!

THE LEVELED-UP HOOK ACRONYM

When writing the hook of your lesson, use one or more of these methods to grab the attention of your students. Use the acronym PLAY to help you remember the different kinds of strategies you can use when writing and planning the hook for your lesson.

P – Personalize: Start your lesson with a personal story or example that connects with what you know about your students. By sharing a personal example or observation, you invite students to reflect on their own life experiences. It could be something funny that happened to you recently, a challenge you overcame, a shared hobby, or even a peek into who you are outside of the classroom. By weaving a personal touch into your lesson, you create an immediate connection with your students and set a positive tone in your classroom.

L – Lure: Begin your lesson with a captivating element that sets the stage for what is being taught. Use a question that students can ponder, a visual hook that intrigues them, a video that invites them to think deeply, or use a surprising fact that interests the class as a whole. When a lesson begins with an element of interest, it will likely open the door for new and exciting learning opportunities for all involved.

A – Activate: Get your students thinking about what they already know or have them become curious about what they are going to learn right from the start. Use an activity that requires students to collaborate, move around the room, or work with a partner. Or have students interact together through role-playing, using manipulatives, solving a challenge, or starting a discussion. Starting a lesson by getting students moving or working together is a great way to foster classroom collaboration.

Y – Yield: Yield to creativity and fun! This type of hook would encompass the themed-based hooks. Let your imagination take the lead as you craft hooks that kick off your lesson with a bit of innovation. Don't be scared to think differently and brainstorm ways to turn your classroom into an exciting adventure. With storytelling, games, and hands-on activities, you will aim to make the lessons unforgettable. This type of hook is just the stepping stone to a memorable lesson and day.

WRITING YOUR HOOK

Learning objectives set the stage by informing students about what they are expected to learn by the end of the lesson. These objectives should be concise and targeted, providing a clear direction for both the teacher and students. Objectives should always be communicated within the first few minutes of the class to help establish expectations and guide students on where to focus their attention most appropriately.

Simultaneously, engaging hooks serve to capture the attention of the students' interests and curiosities. A well-planned hook is like the opening scene of a movie: It grabs the attention and sets the tone for what's to come. Whether it's a thought-provoking question, a surprising fact, a brief activity, or a short story, the hook should be directly tied to the learning objective and resonate with the lesson's main goal. Despite their importance, hooks should be brief. Aiming for just a few minutes, hooks should help to transition into the deeper content of the lesson.

By integrating objectives and hooks, teachers create a dynamic and efficient opening for their lessons. This will enhance student engagement without detracting from the time needed for deeper exploration and practice of the subject matter.

Having delved into the importance of hooks and the various types you can include in your lessons, let's streamline the process of creating a hook for your lesson plan. By following these simple steps, you can efficiently write a hook that not only captures the attention of your students but also integrates with your educational objectives. Never underestimate the power of an engaging lesson hook!

- **Identify the key concept**: Start by reviewing the objective of your lesson to ensure your hook will be relevant and focused.
- **Know your audience**: Tailor your hook to the interests, ages, and cultural backgrounds of your students to maximize engagement.
- **Choose the hook type**: Remember the PLAY acronym? Choose a hook that is either personalized, lures your students in, activates thinking and movement, or yields to creativity and fun.
- **Keep it brief**: While the hook is part of your lesson, it is not the main bulk of your lesson! Aim for a balance of capturing your student's attention and dedicating the time needed to core content.

LEVELED-UP LESSON HOOK IDEAS

Need help spicing up your lesson hooks? Try incorporating one of these suggestions and watch your students' enthusiasm for learning soar! These simple, yet effective ideas are designed to grab attention and light up your learners.

- **Conduct a survey**: Create your survey before the lesson. Write the options on the whiteboard. Give all students a sticky note and let them decide on their choice for the survey. With a survey, there isn't necessarily a right or wrong answer, you are just gathering data. Allow students to place their sticky notes under the answer they agree with most. After, do a quick discussion about the data from the survey before moving into the lesson.
- **Two truths and a lie**: Present three statements to the class that are related to the lesson's topic. Two of the statements should be true, and one should be false. Allow students to discuss with a partner what they think the false statement is and encourage them to think critically about the subject matter. Then talk as a whole group about which statement was false.
- **Museum walk**: Gather different images, infographics, maps, 3D models, charts, or data about the topic being discussed. Arrange them in various locations around the classroom. Students will then walk around the classroom to the different "exhibits" and take notes or make observations about how they are related. Students can also ask questions they are wondering about with each exhibit. When finished, discuss the observations and questions as a class.
- **Play a game**: Students love a little competition! Play a round of bingo, I Have/Who Has, board games, or digital games. Games that are collaborative will also help build teamwork.
- **Videos**: With the Internet nowadays, finding a video for any topic is relatively easy. Playing a short video can capture the attention of your students and set the stage for deeper exploration of a topic. If a video is being used as a lesson hook, make sure it is relevant to the topic and not too long. A good video hook would be between two and five minutes.

- **Sound or music**: Using sounds or music as a lesson hook not only can introduce emotions and feelings for a lesson but can also provide a catchy way to remember content. Allow students to listen to the sound or music a couple of times, once while just reflecting on what they are hearing and a second time taking notes about how the sounds or lyrics make them feel.

- **Riddle**: Get your class thinking critically and problem solving right from the start of your lesson! This method for a lesson hook engages students by challenging them to solve a riddle or puzzle that relates to the lesson topic. From the beginning of your lesson, students will be feeling a sense of accomplishment and anticipation. You can have students work on the riddle independently, with a partner, or with a small group. Gather the class back together to review what the answer to the riddle is, before moving on.

- **Dress up**: If you are planning a themed day, consider dressing up to go along with the lesson theme. You could become a character in a book, historical figure, scientist, inventor, pop icon, or famous person. By dressing up, you create a memorable entry point into the lesson that helps students connect the material in a fun and meaningful way.

- **Food for thought**: Are you starting a new unit where students will need background knowledge of a specific culture or location from around the world? Trying food can be an interesting place to begin! Of course, before bringing food into your classroom, check for allergies, and consider sending a permission slip home to parents so they know students will be having food in class.

- **Hidden treasure**: Have a treasure box in your classroom with an object inside that relates to the lesson. If you don't have a treasure box, using a simple paper lunch bag, or box will work too! Allow students to feel and touch what is inside without looking inside. They can try to guess what the object is just by feeling it. When finished, pull the object out and explain why it is important to the lesson.

CHAPTER 4

Map Expansion: The Introduction of New Material

Have you ever had to learn a new skill and it ended up being much harder than you anticipated? How did you learn the skill without getting frustrated or giving up? When I was a young student, math was always a daunting subject for me. My earliest memories of any type of struggle with school centered around math. As it turns out, I was actually a really great student who loved school, but math was always a challenge.

In fourth grade, we would do timed tests on multiplication facts. We would have to finish an entire page in a specified amount of time before moving on to the next set. This took much effort on my end to accomplish. In fact, my teacher gave me timed tests to practice at home. My parents made copies and each night would test me on my facts. I also had flashcards and little computer games to help me practice my facts. Eventually, I mastered my facts, but it did not come easily. It took a lot of practice and repetition. I am grateful for parents and teachers who didn't give up on me!

Imagine my surprise when in sixth grade I was invited to be in the accelerated math class. "Me? Accelerated math? No way!" This felt like such an honor in my little 11-year-old brain, that I couldn't pass up the opportunity. Plus, I had studied and spent most of my after-school homework time on math, so I felt like I had earned this prestigious invitation.

While I don't remember anything particularly groundbreaking in that class, I do remember finishing sixth grade, entering middle school in seventh grade, and thinking I couldn't do the hard math classes. Maybe I had become intimidated. Maybe I was scared of a challenge. Whatever the case, the euphoria of excelling in math was short-lived. The struggle continued through high school.

I didn't get bad grades in math; I just had to work harder for good ones. While English and literature classes came naturally, math never did. A poignant memory of math in high school was in my junior year. I was in a precalculus class. No matter how hard I tried, I could not wrap my brain around the concepts being taught. I spent time after school with my teacher getting tutored and asking multiple friends for help. Eventually, it was the end of the trimester and we were having a chapter test. I ended up getting a C- on the test. This was one of the lowest grades I had ever received on any test, and I was devastated. I could settle for Bs occasionally, but a C, even worse, a C-, was heartbreaking. Quite nervously, I approached my teacher and asked if I could retake the test. I will always appreciate this teacher's response. She went over the test with me, showed me what I got wrong, helped me better understand the concepts, and then allowed me to study and retake the test. While I didn't get an A, after retaking the test, I did get a B! This teacher believed in me and helped me understand that achieving progress is often better than finding perfection.

The irony of this story is, as I went on to become an elementary sixth-grade teacher, my favorite subject to teach was math. I often had students and parents tell me, "You teach math so well, I (or, my student) understands it so much better in your class." Maybe it was because I struggled with math myself growing up, so I wanted to instill a love of the subject and kick out any doubt from student's minds that I made math fun and engaging instead of intimidating and unachievable. Maybe it was because I worked incredibly hard mastering math myself that I felt confident teaching it. Whatever the case, I always approached math the way I was taught it: It's okay to make mistakes, but it's not okay to give up and never learn from our mistakes. I also had to embrace that fact that I learned from my high school teacher that, often, progress is better than perfection. I didn't have to be perfect in math, but I needed to continue to make progress. This was a motto I tried hard to instill in my students as well.

Let's contrast this with other learning experiences I had growing up because all students should have the opportunity to find joy in their learning, too. In fact, I love learning and realize that is probably part of the reason I have such a passion for teaching! Reading and language arts were always my favorite subjects as a young student. Reading has been something I have enjoyed even from my earliest days as a child. Whether it was my mom reading me a story, or as I got older, reading books on my own, escaping into a new story has been a hobby I have enjoyed for as long as I can remember.

When I was in elementary school, I remember talking with my friend Whitney about a new book, and she told me I had to read it immediately. She raved about the story and said it was the best book she had ever read. I took her word for it and asked my school librarian if she had a copy of *Harry Potter and the Sorcerer's Stone*. The librarian looked at me curiously and said, "I have never heard of that book before. It looks like we don't have it in our library." Now, you're probably thinking, "How in the world did someone not know about Harry Potter?!" This was 1998, and Harry Potter was very new.

Eventually, I begged my dad to take me to Barnes and Noble. While there, I noticed there was a second book as well. My dad told me if I read the first book and liked it, we could come back for the second book. Needless to say, we went back for the second book. It wasn't until I was in college that the last Harry Potter book was released. I even went to the midnight release event and purchased a copy. My sister and I had to each buy our own copies because we weren't about to wait for the other one to finish reading the book (and risk spoiling it) before we could get to it. I was, and still am, a very devoted fan. Those books changed my life. They helped me find an even larger love for reading. As I taught school, I often shared that love of reading by reading aloud the first Harry Potter book to my students.

All this to say, reading hasn't often frustrated me. I even do it in my free time unlike math. Reading and language arts came naturally to me. My favorite class in high school was AP English. I gained a great appreciation for classic literature in that class for writers like Shakespeare and Dostoevsky. Could it be that math became one of my favorite subjects to teach because I had to overcome such hardships with it throughout my learning career? I loved sharing my passion for reading with students, but when I have deeply reflected on my teaching, math truly was my favorite subject to teach, and the one I excelled in the most as a teacher. In fact, math still is my favorite subject to create resources for, even today.

How can we effectively introduce new, challenging, or unfamiliar topics to students in a direct and engaging manner? Every lesson presents the challenge of catering to a diverse classroom where some students may have a natural affinity for the subject, while others may find it frustrating. As educators, we must develop the skill of a "Lesson Plan Magician," creating lessons that captivate and appeal to all students. This essential skill, often not covered in college, is crucial for effective teaching. It is one teachers often learn when thrown into the field on their own.

No one prepares teachers for the reality of addressing such a wide range of learning styles and interests. Yet, this is where the true art of teaching comes into play: transforming potentially daunting subjects into accessible and exciting learning experiences. It's not just about delivering content; it's about engaging hearts and minds and making material resonate with every student regardless of their initial reaction to the subject.

In this chapter, I will provide you with a wealth of strategies to enhance your direct instruction techniques. We will also explore innovative approaches and creative methods to make your lessons more dynamic and interactive. By the end, you will be equipped with the tools to turn even the most complex or unfamiliar topics into lessons that are not only educational but also enjoyable for both you and your students. Let's transform the way we introduce new material and level up our instruction!

As you are "expanding the map of your students' knowledge," you are giving them new information and usually presenting it in a direct instruction type of format. Often, direct instruction is not the sole method of instruction and in my opinion never should be. That is why, in subsequent chapters, we will focus on the other elements to level up a lesson plan, involving guided practice, collaborative practice, and assessment.

While you may use direct instruction during the main portion of your lessons, another method to consider is inquiry-based learning

(IBL). This is an approach that places emphasis on the learner's active engagement in the learning process through questioning, exploring, and investigating topics to deepen their understanding or construct new knowledge. However, without a foundation of the topic, IBL can often be a struggle for some students who don't naturally know how to solve problems on their own. Learning to be a good inquiry-based learner takes practice and guidance. A healthy balance between direct instruction and inquiry instruction can play out to create a wonderful "map expansion of knowledge" for students. Plus, learning one way all the time can be boring! So, during this point in your lesson, you might find yourself doing direct instruction, you might do IBL, or you might do both! Let's break them down together, as well as go over the Map Expansion Roadmap to Success to see the steps you can follow to create engaging, and enjoyable lessons.

DIRECT INSTRUCTION

It is important to build a solid foundation of any topic with your students through direct instruction. This doesn't necessarily mean you need to be lecturing students, but you are laying out the information, showing the steps of a process, and summarizing key ideas. Throughout this process, students should still be actively involved as they work through problems with the teacher and their classmates. This step is important for students, so they have the tools necessary to delve into inquiry-based activities. Think of delivering content to your students like building the perfect ice cream sundae. First, you start with a rich and creamy base of ice cream (direct instruction). Next, you add a layer of delicious toppings like sprinkles, nuts, and fruit (IBL). Last, you finish the sundae with a drizzle of warm chocolate syrup and a cherry on top (engaging exploration). A sundae with just ice cream wouldn't be nearly as delicious or satisfying without all the toppings. Likewise, having the same sundae each day would quickly become monotonous. As educators, it is important to mix our methods of teaching to cater to our students and their needs. Sometimes, they need an extra scoop of ice cream to add to their base of knowledge, while other times adding a few more sprinkles may be the ticket to success.

What is direct instruction, and what is its purpose?

Direct instruction is essential in many scenarios to help ensure students have a clear and thorough understanding of foundational and basic concepts. For example, if a concept needs to be memorized rather than thought about, direct instruction would be the best route. When introducing the principles of multiplication in mathematics, direct instruction helps build a solid base of knowledge. Direct instruction is also important when providing background information. For instance, teaching about a historical event before reading more about it in a book provides the necessary foundation for students when exploring historical events. Students are then set up for success to fully engage with the reading material because they have directly been given information about the event before the reading.

Further examples of direct instruction include the following:

- Introducing the water cycle and using a slide presentation with diagrams
- Demonstrating how to plant a seed in a small cup with soil while explaining all the steps along the way
- Guiding students through basic addition problems on the whiteboard, and talking through each step as you go
- Explicitly teaching how to write a paragraph by going through the different parts of the topic sentence, supporting details, and conclusion
- Modeling fluent reading by reading a story aloud to your class with expressive tones
- Giving step-by-step instructions on how to solve a three-digit subtraction problem by walking through each step aloud with students
- Learning about lifecycles and using pictures and charts to show the lifecycle of a butterfly
- Thinking aloud when teaching about shapes and highlighting and labeling the different parts of each shape
- Demonstrating how to count money while making a pretend purchase and modeling how to do so
- Asking targeted questions while teaching about habitats to check for understanding

One key purpose of direct instruction is to reduce ambiguity and confusion for students. We don't want them to be frustrated in their learning or have them feel like they are failing. There should be a balance between building the knowledge base and exploration, and that is where direct instruction becomes important. When teachers use direct instruction, they break down complex information into manageable steps and provide a clear path for students to follow. In turn, this helps students build their confidence and reduces the chance they will have misconceptions of the topic in the future.

Direct instruction also offers the perfect opportunity for teachers to model the desired skill or behavior expected. For instance, when learning to write an essay, a teacher would model the steps needed for students to follow. This would give students a framework to follow. While experimentation is important, some topics really are taught best directly.

INQUIRY-BASED LEARNING

What is inquiry-based learning (IBL), and what is its purpose?

IBL is a method that allows the student to take control of their learning. It actually works in reverse, compared to direct instruction. Students are presented with a problem and are asked to come up with their own solutions. This fosters critical thinking skills, as well as research skills, since students are tasked with doing a large chunk of the problem-solving. IBL can also encourage intrinsic motivation. When students are tasked with solving a problem, they will pursue methods to fix it that interest them best. This will more likely help them engage in the material. With inquiry-based learning, students also may feel a sense of control. This can be good for students who need to feel a sense of meaning in their work. This type of learning helps them feel purpose.

Here are further examples of IBL:

- Conduct a plant growth experiment where students test how different variables, like light, soil, and water, affect plant growth.

- Keeping a weather journal, students document the weather each day for a month and then make predictions based on their data.
- Create a research report on animal habitats where students choose an animal to learn about and present the information they find to the class.
- Build a simple machine students can test and explore different mechanisms and how they work.
- After collecting various rocks, students can study their differences and make classifications based on their findings.
- Give students materials like sand, soil, rocks, plastic wrap, and containers of varying sizes. Then, have students conduct experiments modeling how the water cycle works.
- Students can create models of the solar system after researching the characteristics of each planet.
- Have students create a density experiment where they test various objects and observe if and why they float or do not float.
- Test different materials using magnets, and have students keep a journal of their observations and experiments.
- Start your math lesson by asking, "How can math be useful in our everyday lives?" Then, encourage students to explore ways, and discuss with small groups, how math is useful in their lives.

IBL has a myriad of benefits that can help students of all backgrounds. Like stated earlier, it helps students develop problem-solving skills, but more than that, it encourages creativity. As students are given the opportunity to explore a question or topic, they often come up with creative solutions all on their own. This is because they are not restricted on how to solve the problem, and they are just asked to solve it in any way that they can.

This type of learning can also teach great communication skills. In an ever growing world of screens and online networking, getting students to learn to work face-to-face is crucial. While working to solve a problem in a small group, students are often tasked with explaining their thoughts and ideas to others. As students work together, and debate on their reasonings, they are learning to engage correctly with other people.

EXPANDING THE KNOWLEDGE MAP WITH DIRECT INSTRUCTION AND INQUIRY-BASED LEARNING

Direct instruction usually feels "easier" and may come more naturally to most people. So, how do we flawlessly combine direct instruction and IBL to expand our student's map of knowledge and level up their learning? At this point in your lesson, you are introducing new material. Some students pick things up from experiencing them or through activities, while others will need face-to-face instruction. The key is to know your students and know how much background knowledge they have on the topic before deciding how you will expand their knowledge base in the map expansion phase.

Creating an effective learning environment should actually blend both direct instruction and IBL. Setting the solid foundation of information and then guiding students to find the answers can create a classroom environment that allows for learning at all levels. By combining these two methods, teachers can address the diverse needs of their students more effectively, ensuring that everyone benefits from both structured learning and exploratory learning.

Starting a lesson on a completely new topic, while using direct instruction, ensures that all students are given the baseline of essential knowledge and skills they will need to progress. This step is vital in the learning process because it establishes the framework of the topic being presented. For example, during a history lesson, direct instruction helps students grasp the fundamental timelines of events before they dive into research projects or discuss the historical impacts of the events.

Once the foundation is laid, IBL can take over to encourage a deeper understanding of the topics. Students can apply what they learned through direct instruction to real-world scenarios. This will help encourage critical thinking and problem-solving skills. For instance, once the historical events have been taught, students might be given a question like "How did the propaganda influence public opinion during WWII?" Students would then use their background knowledge from the direct instruction phase of the lesson to explore their answers during IBL and collaborative investigation with other classmates.

By blending the two teaching methods of direct instruction and IBL, educators create a dynamic and inclusive learning environment that accepts many different learning styles. The educational experience becomes more engaging and conducive to all involved.

ROADMAP FOR STUDENT MAP EXPANSION

Follow the roadmap in Figure 4.1 for a successful introduction to new material when teaching your students.

Leveled-Up Lesson Map Expansion Ideas

Looking to refresh and rejuvenate your direct instruction and IBL segments of your lesson? Experiment with one of these suggestions and watch your students' comprehension and enthusiasm skyrocket! These straightforward yet powerful techniques are created to grab attention and enrich learning.

- **Graphic organizers**: When presenting new information, helping students organize it efficiently can also guide them in remembering the topic better. Provide graphic organizers and diagrams for students to use and take notes.
- **Stop and think**: Break up your instruction into 5–10-minute intervals. During each stopping point, have students think of one thing they just learned during the lesson and share it with a partner.
- **Corner quiz**: Assign each corner of your room a letter A–D. Every 10 minutes or so, during your lesson, ask a question and give four multiple-choice answers. Each choice will correspond with a letter in a corner of the room. Students will move to the corner they feel best represents the answer to your question.
- **Boil it down**: When you have finished presenting the information to the class, have students get in a group and write a 40-word summary. Then they are to pass their summary to another group who edits their summary to 30 words. Next, the summary is passed to another group who edits it down to 20 words. Share the summaries with the class.

- **Beach ball pass**: Write questions on a beach ball that are related to your lesson. At the end of instruction, have students sit in a circle and pass the ball around. Whoever catches the ball reads and answers one of the questions on the ball.
- **Design challenges**: Pose a problem related to your lesson and give students materials to design an object, tool, or idea to solve the problem.
- **Trivia challenge**: Create 10–15 questions that relate to the lesson being taught. At the end, divide your class into teams and see which team can answer the questions correctly first.
- **Board game creation**: After direct instruction is complete, have students create a board game that reviews the skills they were taught. Then, they can play their games with a partner.
- **Story add-on**: Write a story as a whole class that relates to the topic of the lesson. The teacher will begin with a starting sentence and then call on students to add to it, one sentence at a time.
- **Hurrah/boo**: During your lesson pause occasionally make a statement about the topic being introduced (true or false) to check for understanding. Students are to shout, "Hurrah!" if the statement is true, and "Boo!" if the statement is false.

FIGURE 4.1   When introducing new material

CHAPTER 5

Join the Training Arena During Guided Practice

Guided practice is the bridge that connects effective teaching methods of introducing material to independent student work. During this phase of the Leveled-Up Lesson Plan, teachers can model concepts, provide support in a structured environment, and gradually release responsibility of the tasks to the student. This helps ensure confidence in the students. They are allowed to practice the new skills they are learning, and it is okay if they make mistakes because they have a confident and proficient teacher ready and willing to help when necessary.

During guided practice, teachers frequently witness what we fondly call "the lightbulb moment." You know the one: It's that magical instant when students' faces lights up with comprehension, when the fog of confusion clears, and when they truly grasp the concept they are learning. This moment is not just about understanding the material but recognizing how the steps align, work together, and can be interpreted.

This is a pivotal shift in a student's journey. They start to believe in their own abilities and are willing to take greater risks in their learning. The student is now controlling their learning in a more intrinsic way, rather than just gathering information to store in their knowledge of understanding.

As a teacher, there was nothing I loved more than seeing the lightbulb moment occur. It was what I lived for each day. In my opinion, great teachers cultivate a classroom environment where such moments are not rare but are actually daily experiences that guide their students through fundamental learning breakthroughs.

Do you have many memories from elementary school? Probably not. Most likely, you remember more of how you felt in those years than the moments you experienced. Those moments were pivotal in your learning and growing experience, yet isn't it interesting that you don't remember much of what was experienced? To be honest, I have only a few vivid memories that really stand out (a few of which I have shared in this book). However, these pivotal memories often involve at least one of the following: an important milestone in my life, an event that changed me, or a teacher who impacted my life.

One of these moments occurred in sixth grade with one of my all-time favorite teachers, Mrs. Anderson. Mrs. Anderson was the kind of teacher who made every student feel loved and included. In fact, she is one of my major inspirations for becoming a teacher myself. For one writing activity in her class, I even drew a picture of myself dreaming I could be a teacher (the irony is I went on to be a sixth-grade teacher myself); see Figure 5.1.

I never knew I enjoyed writing or even had any talent for it until I entered sixth grade. That's when Mrs. Anderson introduced us to the concept of keeping journals. Every day, we were expected to write in our journals, sometimes following a given topic, sometimes writing freely about whatever came to mind. The routine was simple: We would arrive at school in the morning, put our bags away, and spend 10—15 minutes writing. I remember at the beginning of the year it felt like a grueling task. How was I ever going to write continually for 15 minutes? However, with time, it became easier and easier.

What truly captivated me about this activity, though, wasn't even the act of writing. Each month, we would hand in our journals to Mrs. Anderson, who would then read through our entries and respond to our writing. It wasn't just a generic response either; she engaged with us on a personal level. I distinctly remember writing her questions in my journal and eagerly awaiting her answers. This practice showcased her devotion to her students. She wasn't just teaching us; she was building a connection and fostering a love for writing.

FIGURE 5.1 My sixth-grade assignment

Through the process, Mrs. Anderson could closely monitor our writing progress. Her responses often included suggestions for improvement and examples of excellent writing, providing us with a model to aspire to. This daily routine not only improved our writing skills but also strengthened our bond with our teacher. Mrs. Anderson's dedication and personal touch turned a simple journaling exercise into a transformative experience that ignited a love of learning and growing within me.

My experience with journaling in sixth grade can be closely compared to the guided practice portion of a lesson. Guided practice is a key moment in the lesson. This is the point where students apply new skills and knowledge with the teacher's support and feedback. Just as guided practice is designed to bridge the gap between instruction and independent work, our daily journal writing served as a scaffolded learning activity that provided continuous guidance and feedback.

Each morning, when we dedicated time to our journals, it was similar to engaging in guided practice. Our teacher set clear expectations and often provided prompts for our writing, much like a teacher would provide structured tasks during guided practice. This daily routine allowed us to practice our writing regularly, reinforcing the skills and concepts she taught. The consistency helped us develop our writing abilities incrementally, mirroring the step-by-step approach of guided practice.

The monthly feedback we received from Mrs. Anderson was similar to the immediate and specific feedback given during the guided practice phase of a lesson plan. This interaction was critical to our growth as writers. Her personalized feedback helped us understand our strengths and areas for improvement, much like a teacher's role during guided practice is to provide corrective feedback and reinforce the learning objectives.

Last, Mrs. Anderson's responses in our journals served as examples of good writing, similar to how teachers model skills before and during guided practice. By reading her responses, we could see firsthand what effective writing looked like. This modeling helped us learn effective writing techniques and strategies, making the journaling a dynamic and interactive form of guided practice. Her engagement with our writing not only enhanced our skills but helped us, as students, create deeper connections in the learning process.

In this chapter, we will break the guided practice portion of your lesson into three sections: modeling, guidance, and independent practice. Each of these sections plays a part in helping students build a strong foundation of understanding and skills. By structuring the guided practice section of your lesson this way, you can help students receive the support they need at each stage of the learning process and ideally capture those lightbulb moments in action! This will also, ideally, lead to greater independence and confidence in their abilities to learn and put their knowledge to work.

Modeling involves the teacher demonstrating new skills or new concepts in a clear and structured manner. During this phase, the teacher showcases the steps and thought process involved in mastering the task. This provides students with a concrete example to follow and helps clarify any misconceptions they may have. By observing the teacher's example, students begin to form a mental framework of what they must do to replicate the process on their own.

Next, guidance transitions students from observation to becoming an active participant in their learning. The teacher is providing support when necessary but is watching the student progress on their own. The goal is to gradually release responsibility to the student, allowing them to practice increasing levels of independence. That brings us to the independent portion, of the guided practice part, of the lesson. This stage is essential for reinforcing learning and ensuring that students can perform the skill on their own. Students apply what they have learned without teacher help. The ultimate goal is for the student to master the topic proficiently. Let's break down each section a little more thoroughly.

MODELING

Have you ever tried to perform a task without knowing how to do it? What would that be like? For example, I have never built a desk from scratch; however, my husband is an experienced woodworker and has built furniture for our home! If I wanted to build a desk, without any background knowledge or information, without anyone showing me the tools I needed or the materials, without reading instructions or any guidance at all, I would be completely lost. The task would seem overwhelming and insurmountable.

I would have so many questions. What kind of wood should I use? What tools do I need? How and what do I measure? Without this basic knowledge, I become stuck. Every step is guesswork and frustration.

My experience learning to build an office desk would be vastly different with the guidance of someone with experience. With a mentor or teacher knowledgeable on the subject, I could be guided in the right direction. I would learn which tools to use, materials to buy, and how to put them all together. The task would feel manageable, and I would feel confident knowing I had someone I could bounce ideas off of until I felt ready to do the task on my own.

Now imagine students who are tasked with a learning objective but are not shown or modeled how it is to be done. Day after day, this would become an incredibly difficult way to live. This is why modeling is essential in our lesson plans. As students join the training arena of learning, they need to be given instructions and tools to feel up to the responsibility.

Consider how this teacher models a simple math topic with her students. This portion of the lesson doesn't need to be fancy or intense; it just needs to be understandable.

In Miss Harper's kindergarten classroom, the students were settled onto the carpet, ready for their math lesson. Miss Harper stood at her whiteboard and had her hand full of colorful markers. She announced to her class, "Today, we're going to learn about addition." She began with something simple and drew one apple on the board. Miss Harper said, "If I drew another apple next to my first one, I now have two apples!" She then pointed to each apple as she counted, and said, "1, 2! One plus one equals two. Addition is like counting up!"

At this point, Miss Harper can continue modeling a few more sample questions. As she goes, she can make them slightly more difficult. Maybe modeling two plus one, or three plus two. Miss Harper continued, "We have three apples here and if we add two more, how many do we have now?" She pointed to each apple, counted them aloud, and said, "5!" As the teacher explains her thinking aloud and points to her images on the board, she is modeling addition to her students. Miss Harper can expand on this and make the lesson more engaging by inviting volunteers to come up to the board and draw their own objects on the board, like stars or balls, and create simple addition problems.

Modeling provides students with a clear picture of what the outcome of their task should be. It shows them how to find success. There are many different effective ways to model your instruction in your classroom, but modeling is more than just demonstrating a task to your students and having them observe your actions; it should include the students in the process. We aren't just telling student information when we model; we are describing it for deeper understanding.

Here are some great tips for modeling with your students:

- **Use visuals**: Show students how a concept works by using visual aids. For instance, when teaching how the fractions ½ and 2/4 are equivalent, a teacher could use fraction circles and layer them on top of each other. The teacher is modeling that the fractions are the same size and are equivalent.
- **Think out loud**: Narrate what you are thinking and doing as you complete the objective being taught. For example, "As I look at this multiplication problem 3×4, I can see there are three groups of 4. I am going to draw a picture to show my thinking. Now I know, 3×4 equals 12."
- **Ask questions**: As you model, ask questions to help students understand thinking deeply. As an example, imagine you are reading a Robert Frost poem with your fifth-grade students. You can model how to understand the poem and what the author is saying by asking "What do you think the line 'I took the one less traveled by, and that has made all the difference,' means?"
- **Show a video**: In a world filled with technology, why not use it? Showing a video to model what is being learned is one strategy that can help get your students focused and engaged.
- **Complete the first one**: When giving students a set of problems or questions to answer, complete the first one in the set. Put the question on the board or under the document camera and model how to accurately complete it. This way, as students begin working on their own, they have a question to refer to.
- **Break it down**: When teaching and modeling a more complex topic, consider breaking it down into smaller pieces. Introduce one step or piece at a time.

Some may be concerned that modeling for your students can make learning less complex and "too easy." However, I would like to counter that while it might make it easier for students to learn a concept when a teacher models it, it does not make the task any less complex. In fact, when modeling is done efficiently by a teacher, students will be confident in their work going forward and can solve different but similar tasks because they have accurate background knowledge to complete their work.

GUIDANCE

After teachers have effectively modeled what they are teaching, the next step is to gradually shift the responsibility to the students. Essentially, guided practice allows students to work through newly learned skills with the help of an observing teacher. Students may even be working in small groups or with a partner as they work to continue to comprehend what is being taught. However, the teacher is still always observing and giving feedback during this guidance stage.

Going back to the desk building example from earlier, if I were to tackle this project after my mentor has taught me what tools I need to use and how to execute the project, the next step would be to build. After some modeling and explanation, I would ideally be confident enough to begin building the desk. With a mentor's help, watching each step and giving feedback when necessary, I can be confident that my desk will turn out the way it needs. While I am still doing the work with the observation of a teacher, I can have more guarantees that I will find success quickly and efficiently.

Imagine you are teaching a lesson to a group of third-grade students about writing opinions with supporting details. After showing examples and modeling, including writing samples for the class, it is time to have students write and create their own opinion sentences with supporting reasons and details.

For instance, the teacher may say to her class, "I think school lunches should include more fruit options. What do you think? Talk with a partner and write down three reasons to support this opinion." Then, after students discuss with a partner, students would share their examples with the class.

At this point in the lesson, students are still not fully doing the assignment on their own. They have worked with a partner and then shared ideas with the teacher. The teacher can go over the ideas shared and explain why they work for the opinion being stated. Eventually, a teacher would want to have the students write their own opinions and create their own reasons to support their ideas; however, that is the last step in guided practice. For now, students have been given a model and are gradually taking over responsibility for their learning.

What are some fun ways you can level up your guided practice portion of your lesson? Here are a few examples:

- **Graphic organizers**: After introducing a graphic organizer with your students and showing them how it is to be used, encourage them to complete it. As they complete it, they can work with a partner or ask for assistance from the teacher if needed.
- **Group brainstorming**: With this method of guided practice, you would start your discussion with a question or prompt. Then, as a group, students can generate ideas working through a concept together. Finally, students can categorize their brainstorming session and group similar ideas together, rank them or evaluate them individually.
- **Using manipulatives**: Having students use something tangible and interactive can help them deepen their understanding of a topic that might be more abstract. For instance, fraction circles are a great way to help students visualize parts of a whole and show how different fractions compare to each other.
- **Role-play**: If a lesson is being taught and students can role-play characters, this is a fun way to enhance your guided practice portion of the lesson. Consider using reader's theaters or even just have students act out specific pieces of a lesson.

If you haven't guessed it already, the guided practice portion of any lesson is a critical phase of the learning process for students. After they have been introduced to new material, they are slowly shown how to apply their knowledge with the guidance of their teacher. During guided practice, the role of the teacher changes from being the primary source of knowledge and expertise to that of a coach or mentor. Teachers can move around the classroom and observe their students putting their learning into action. As they do this, teachers can give immediate feedback and critique student learning as necessary. It may even become apparent that the teacher will pause the whole class and return to modeling and teaching the concept if they find a lot of their students are asking the same question or struggling with a particular concept.

Guided practice is also an excellent chance for teachers to incorporate collaborative learning and allow students to work in pairs or groups. This allows students to share their knowledge with their peers and even tutor each other if needed. Sometimes, hearing the information from a peer does wonders for another student's learning! By creating a supportive atmosphere where students are comfortable sharing their ideas and making mistakes, teachers help to build a classroom culture that values growth and learning, making guided practice a powerful tool in a teacher's toolbox of learning.

INDEPENDENT PRACTICE

When students are in the Training Arena and have been given the tools needed to learn a topic, eventually, they will be led to independent practice. However, independent practice cannot occur when a new skill is taught, until the previous steps of modeling and guided practice have been completed. Otherwise, students will not have the knowledge or experience to confidently complete their tasks.

Take, for example, this scenario: Mr. Foster is teaching his fifth-grade students about decimal place value. He feels a bit behind and is trying to catch up for the day in his lessons. He briefly shows the students a place value table for decimals but doesn't accurately model or explain the difference between the tenths and hundredths place. A few minutes later, he hands out a worksheet for students to name the decimals given. Mr. Foster thinks showing the students the table of decimal place value and leaving it up on the board for all to see, will be enough to introduce decimals and their value. Many students struggle. A couple even give up and put their heads on their desk. Mr. Foster is discouraged and frustrated as he notices that most of his students are asking questions and many seem confused. Now, Mr. Foster will be even further behind in his lessons as he determines he needs to revisit the topic.

This could have been remedied by simply modeling decimal place value appropriately the first time and then gradually releasing the students to take questions on their own. He could have modeled what decimals were and the value of each place and even allowed students to use manipulatives as they practiced questions that gradually increased in difficulty, together.

It is essential to model new learning objectives appropriately. Otherwise, precious learning time is wasted. It is also realistic to note, in a class full of students learning at all different levels, they will not all grasp the topics at the same time. It is unrealistic to think every student will understand every single subject you teach 100% of the time.

So, how do you know when it is time to transition to independent practice? Independent practice can also be a great chance for differentiation as needed, but we will get to that in a minute! First, students should demonstrate a solid understanding of the material being taught with minimal support from the teacher. If students can complete a task with little assistance, you know your students are approaching their time for independent practice. Understanding of the topic can be demonstrated in a myriad of different ways, whether students are answering questions correctly, explaining their thinking, or applying their knowledge to new situations.

Another way to check to see if your students are ready to work on their own is to check for understanding during the guiding practice phase. As the teacher asks questions or prompts students to explain their thinking, the teacher can gauge how well the students are digesting the information. Teachers can ask open-ended questions that require more than a yes or no answer. For example, instead of asking "Do you understand?" which is vague and can be intimidating (who wants to say no to this question?), a teacher might ask, "Can you explain why you chose your solution?" Or, "What steps did you take to arrive at the answer?" These questions not only help the teacher see if students correctly applied the concept but also reveal any misconceptions or gaps in their thinking.

Lastly, a teacher should also look for consistent performance of the learning objective being taught. If a student answers only one question out of 10 correctly, it's a clear sign they have not accurately mastered the concept enough to do it independently. If students haven't mastered the concept, it is likely they will need to rely on guesswork or partial knowledge rather than a solid understanding. Such inconsistency would highlight the need for further guided practice before the students were turned over to work independently on their own. On the other hand, a student who can consistently perform a particular strategy reliably shows they are developing the correct thinking skills to work independently.

Once you have determined your students are ready for independent practice, it is time to consider what type of work students will do to practice their new skills. Back in the 1900s (I grew up in the '90s!), this meant a lot of worksheets. Like, a lot. I remember my teachers passing out papers constantly, and we would just do pages of work. Did we do some fun learning exercises? Sure but not as often as we probably would have liked. I want to make it clear that I had a wonderful school experience; however, the models for learning have drastically changed. What students need today to be successful has changed. I grew up in a time when tablets and cell phones were nonexistent, and I had every single friend's home landline memorized, not stashed away on an iPhone with my contact list at the ready. Students today need to interact with others, they need to use their hands, they need to be creative, and they need to learn how to think critically and problem solve. During independent practice, this is a wonderful time to implement some of these skills for students to practice.

Let's level up the independent portion of your lesson plan. What are some activities or strategies you can use to get your students excited about learning their new skills?

- **Interactive worksheets**: These are not your normal print-and-go worksheets that are meant to be "busywork" but are meant to get students interacting with the content. Some types of interactive worksheets include puzzles, riddles, and word searches. Want to up the ante a bit more? Try an activity like a color-by-number or cut-and-categorize activity. With the color-by-number, students are solving questions and then coloring portions of the picture to match their answers. This is a great way to get kids thinking, plus adding a bit of fun to their work. With cutting-and-categorizing activities, students might sort vocabulary words, pictures, or spelling words and glue them onto the correct portion of their worksheet.

- **Mystery reveals:** These are a fun way to get students working, too! With these activities, students are given secret codes or tasks that should be finished in sequential order. As they finish each task, a mystery word, answer, or picture is revealed. With this, students are studying a topic, but they are also problem solving. This type of worksheet encourages a deeper connection to the material as students work toward uncovering hidden elements.

- **Digital quests:** One of my favorite forms of review is to use an escape room. In fact, I love them so much that I dedicated a whole chapter in this book to them. However, I will mention them briefly here, too. Digital quests, or escape rooms, are the perfect way to allow students to review content during independent practice. I want to emphasize digital because usually I would suggest the printable escape rooms and quests to be done in groups. Although with digital escape rooms, they can be done in Google Forms, Google Slides, or other programs, and really do lend themselves well to independent learners. Often, the mystery of the game is thrilling for the students and motivates them to continue.

- **Learning stations:** Whether you call them centers, rotations, or stations, this is an excellent method to use for students to review their new skills they are learning. Within your classroom, you will create distinct spaces for different tasks or activities. As students rotate through the stations, they are not only practicing skills but are also learning to manage their time and acquire independent thinking and planning. Being able to navigate through all the stations gives students a sense of responsibility and helps them gain valuable life skills beyond the classroom.

Learning stations are also a great place to integrate different subjects. While you might be doing learning stations during language arts, you could easily incorporate science and social studies reading material. This is a great way to also differentiate learning, which we will touch on later in the chapter.

Here are some basic steps for setting up learning stations in your classroom:

1. Set your objectives. What will your students be practicing at each station? Ideally, they will review topics currently being taught in the classroom. However, having one or two stations that are review from previous lessons, even from earlier in the school year, is a great way to continue practicing important skills.

2. Determine the number of stations you will want to have. This will be based on the amount of time you have set aside for center time. Even for older elementary students in sixth grade I did literacy centers in my classroom. I did three centers a day, each lasting 15–20 minutes. This allowed me to also have one small group at a time that I worked with on extra reading skills. So, we had 45–60 minutes of center time, depending on the day. This was a great way for me to also throw in spelling practice, give students time to work on writing assignments, and allow students to work collaboratively together in some stations. I liked meeting with groups that needed a little extra support while also giving those students who can work independently a chance to practice managing their time.

3. Design the activities you want to use. To make things simple and consistent, I often had the same themes for each of my rotations. I would do Spelling, Writing, Teacher Time, Technology, Grammar, and Reading. Each day I did only three centers; however, they were always one of these topics. I also had specific games, activities, and practice work that would be rotated through the centers so students came to understand how each center worked. I tried to keep the rotation time consistent so students knew what to expect. A schedule that was predictable helped my students be more successful.

4. Create space for each station. You will need to distinguish locations in your classroom for each center. My suggestion would be to keep each station in the same location each time. For example, I always did Teacher Time at the front of the classroom. This way, I could keep an eye on all the other centers, but students also knew where to go when it was their time to work with me.

5. Introduce and model appropriate behavior during center time, plus PRACTICE, PRACTICE, PRACTICE. Before you do any Teacher Time centers, make sure your students have the routines and procedures set. This may take a few weeks, depending on the ages of your students. However, time spent setting up solid routines is well worth its time!

■ **Journaling**: There is more than one way to journal! Of course, students can be given a prompt and asked to write their thoughts. This is an excellent way to practice writing skills and expand on writing capability. However, journaling can be used in other subject areas as well. Here are some journaling examples that can be used in your lessons:

o **Learning logs**: This would be like summarizing notes from different lessons. At the end of each lesson or subject, give students 5–10 minutes to summarize what they have learned. They can detail the topics covered for the day, give examples of what they have learned, or rewrite steps to certain tasks.

o **Interactive notebooks**: This is one of my favorite ways to incorporate journaling in the classroom. Students can include creative elements like folded papers, diagrams, mind maps, and written entries to create notes for any subject.

o **Double-entry journals**: With this method, students draw a line down the middle of a page. On the left side, students take notes about what they are learning from the lesson or their reading. Then, on the right side, students ask questions and reflect or make personal responses. This type of journaling helps students think critically and ask important questions about their learning.

o **Character journals**: This is a type of journaling where students can write from the perspective of someone else. Whether it is a character in a book, a person from history, or a scientist they are studying, this is a fun way to expand learning on different subjects.

o **Creative writing journal**: This type of writing would mean the journal is kept as a place for students to express themselves creatively. Whether it is through short stories, poems, or narratives about what is being studied in class, students can write to make their learning more engaging and personal.

■ **Building and creating**: This strategy for independent practice is a great way to leverage hands-on activities with visual learning to help deepen your students' understanding of complex concepts. After learning a concept and having it be applied to their background knowledge, students can take what they've learned and start using it in real-world situations. For instance, students can create models of the solar system, or animal habitats, to showcase what they know. Or students can visualize their math concepts better creating 3D shapes or using manipulatives to work with fractions.

Building and creating during independent practice can also be as simple as drawing diagrams. Students can sketch diagrams or illustrations to explain the process of solving math problems or can showcase a historical timeline. Putting their knowledge on paper and visualizing it in a new way is a great learning opportunity for the student. Then, students can share their creations with the class, too.

SETTING UP EXPECTATIONS DURING INDEPENDENT PRACTICE

Like any lesson, instruction, or activity in your classroom, having clear expectations makes managing your classroom environment not only easier on you but also more welcoming and conducive to learning for your students. Setting clear rules and expectations during independent practice is especially important because students are working on their own as you monitor the class as whole. They need to be expected to stay on task and work on the assignment given. Not only this, but clear expectations help minimize confusion and disruptions and creates smoother transitions to instructional time. Having clear rules and expectations during independent practice cannot be overstated; these expectations are like a roadmap for students, guiding them through their tasks and helping them understand what they need to do to achieve success.

Here is a basic outline of what your rules and procedures can look like during independent work in your classroom:

1. Start by clearly stating the objective of the independent work. What is the end goal and why? What do you expect students to accomplish?

Make sure students know the purpose of what they are doing, or why else would they be motivated to do it?

2. Set up your behavioral expectations. This is most likely not a time with lots of loud talking. While learning can take place in that sort of environment, if students are working independently, whispering and communication policies should be put in place.

3. Where will students be seated or working? Emphasize the importance of where your students will be working, so you can monitor their progress.

4. Next, consider how resources will be managed. What materials will be used? How will the materials be handled? Make sure these materials are easily accessible and available for all students.

5. Consider implementing a "three before me" rule, where students must try three solutions to their problem before approaching the teacher. This could be trying to solve a problem in a new way, asking other students quietly for help, researching their question on a computer or in a textbook, or some other way. If students still needs help, create a procedure for them to approach you for help during independent work time.

6. Finally, outline what students should do if or when they finish their tasks. Are they to review their work, clean their workspace, move on to a free choice activity, or something else?

My pro tip would be to keep the rules and procedures as consistent as possible for each day. This way, students will be able to come to know what to expect in your classroom and will not need to spend time re-learning different sets of expectations every day. Consistency will not only help reduce confusion but will also aid in building a stable and predictable learning environment. Having a familiarity with routines will promote a sense of security and confidence among your students.

Creating consistency with any of your rules and procedures in your classroom will, in fact, help make transitions between different activities smoother and reduce behavior issues. There is less time to misbehave or not follow classroom rules when students are busy following the clear and outlined procedures that are practiced and set into place each day.

DIFFERENTIATING DURING INDEPENDENT PRACTICE

Not every student approaches independent practice with the same level of confidence. Differentiating is a key concept during this point in your lesson. Fair teaching doesn't imply that all students receive identical information, practice, or tools. Rather, it ensures that all students receive what they need to succeed. During independent practice, students can work at their own pace, addressing their unique needs and skill sets. The challenge lies in ensuring that, despite these differences, all students are striving toward a common objective. It's easier said than done, I know! Been there, done that.

I remember teaching sixth grade and having a range of learners and abilities. Some of my students were reading well above a sixth-grade level, and some were two, three, or even four grades behind. As a relatively new teacher, I found it daunting to devise lessons for 32 students, each with distinct learning styles and abilities that varied widely. How was I supposed to meet such diverse needs in a single classroom? Before I give some suggestions on how to easily differentiate your independent work or lessons in general, I want to make it clear what some common do's and don'ts are when differentiating (see Figure 5.2).

As we dive into ways to differentiate during your lessons, let's explore the differences among these two teachers:

In an elementary school, there are a couple of fourth-grade teachers whose philosophies differ. Each has their strengths; however, one teacher explores the benefits of differentiation, while another does not.

Mrs. Norton's class was often buzzing with activity and quiet conversations. Her walls had bright displays of student projects and instructions for learning stations were clearly hanging on the wall. Mrs. Norton worked hard to differentiate her lessons to meet the needs of her many students, and it was obvious when you entered her classroom. For instance, during a unit on the water cycle, she applied tiered assignments. Tiered assignments allowed her to adjust the intensity of the assignment to meet the needs of all her learners. For example, one group of students wrote an essay about the water cycle and created a slide presentation to go along with it. Another group of students wrote an essay with some guidance from the teacher and followed an outline chart they were provided that

Do's	Don'ts
• **Assess student needs regularly.** Understand their learning styles, interests and educational backgrounds.	• **Use a one-size-fits-all approach.** Avoid assuming all students will benefit from the same assignment or activity.
• **Provide multiple ways to learn.** For example, use strategies like visual aids, hands-on activities, or technology.	• **Overwhelm students with options.** Offering too many choices at once can be confusing and over stimulating.
• **Set clear goals that are achievable.** Make sure that the tasks students are given, are attainable for their work level.	• **Set the same goals for everyone.** Don't expect all students to meet the same academic standards at the same pace.
• **Encourage self-paced learning.** Allow students to progress at their own pace, especially if the work can be adapted for independent study.	• **Rush the learning process.** Don't push students to move forward before they are ready.
• **Use formative assessments.** Use a range of assessment strategies that inform and guide the learning and instructional process.	• **Rely solely on summative assessments.** If you wait until the end of a unit or term to assess students, you will miss critical growth and learning periods.

FIGURE 5.2   Differentiating dos and don'ts

explained the different parts of an essay. The last group of students wrote an essay about the water cycle, with the help and feedback of a teacher. This last group also was required to write three paragraphs, instead of five.

Later in the unit, the students were also asked to create a model to represent the water cycle. However, instead of Mrs. Norton giving all the students the same project, she allowed them to choose from several different options: create a diorama, illustrate a flowchart on a poster, or create a written reader's theater. All options would require students to showcase their knowledge on the water cycle, but they had the opportunity to choose which project to complete. Not only does this allow students to have some independence, but they are also able to choose a project that benefited their strengths and that they felt more confident with.

Contrast this with Mr. Martinez's classroom. Mr. Martinez is an excellent teacher but uses a traditional model when delivering content to his students. Often, you will find him delivering a lecture while students listen quietly. He emphasizes students all learning the same standards, and values consistency within his teaching methods.

While students should all be learning the same standards, the key is differentiating that learning. Also, quiet students don't always translate to listening or understanding students. Mr. Martinez would benefit from allowing students to talk to each other and share ideas. He would also find success by allowing students to try learning the same concepts but in new ways. The problem with Mr. Martinez's traditional approach, while mostly outdated, is that it can also marginalize some groups of students. Traditional lecturing really only helps the middle-tier students or those who are learning and progressing on grade level. It does not benefit gifted students or students who need more support. This is why differentiation is crucial in today's classrooms.

Both of these teachers are great educators who care for their students. However, one will find more success with their student's learning because it is tailored to all of them instead of just a few students. Although, let's not lose hope in Mr. Martinez! With some guidance, he can easily transition his teaching and continue to be the stellar teacher he was meant to be. While differentiation can seem daunting and overwhelming, I am here to show you some fun and easy ways to level up that independent practice with suggestions for differentiation for your students. Let's explore those ways now.

- **Choice boards**: This type of differentiation involves providing a menu of activity or task options related to a specific skill or learning objectives. Each activity targets the same skill, but the choice board allows students to choose how they will demonstrate their understanding of the topic. This differentiates learning because it allows students to choose an activity based on their interest and progress levels.

Choice boards also allow students to work at their own pace. So, if a student needs more time than another student, that is okay! Early finishers can choose a second or third choice from the board to complete. This helps students learn to manage their own time as well.

- **Tiered assignments**: This strategy involves creating multiple versions of the same task or assignment. The purpose is to ensure each student is working on the sameskill, but at a different level of complexity.

Usually, there would be three tiers. A basic tier would be designed for students who are still working on foundational skills or need extra support from the teacher. An intermediate tier would be for students who have a basic understanding of the skill being taught but might just need a bit more practice to solidify the concepts. The advanced tier is for students who have clearly mastered the topic and are ready for more complex or higher-order thinking tasks.

The final demonstration of learning may differ, but all students are concentrating on the same skill. Tiered assignments allow teachers to meet the needs of all of their students by providing the right amount of challenge and work, without being overwhelming. Tiered assignments also help eliminate boredom and frustration. All students is are working in their own zone of development, while still learning and being challenged.

- **Flexible grouping**: This type of differentiation focuses on grouping students for various reasons. You may group students based on factors like learning needs, on their interests, or as peer support groups. The type of flexible groups you create would depend on the type of lesson you are teaching and the desired outcome you want. Do you want students to practice a skill they have already been taught a few times? Then grouping students based on interests might work well. Are you grouping students based on a new skill being taught? Then grouping on ability level would be my first suggestion. Focusing on test prep? Consider grouping students in peer groups where some students can help guide other students in the group.

Flexible grouping is a great method to use during independent practice. For example, if you are grouping students based on skill level during a math lesson on fractions, you might assign different types of math problems to different sets of students. While they are working independently on different assignments, they are grouped in your lesson because you have given different tasks for them to complete.

Interest-based grouping is a nice strategy because students can all work on similar skills but focus on what they like. For instance, with writing, you might be having students write about a historical event you are learning in class. Some students might enjoy writing fiction and will create a story that is based in the time period of the historical event being learned. Then there might be students who prefer informational text and will be writing a detailed report with a timeline about the history being learned.

Peer support groups can even work well during independent practice! You can pair students together or put them in groups where you have students that have a strong grasp of the concept, matched with those who might still be struggling, even though the students will be working independently. The students can be asked to check in with each other to ask questions, share strategies, or give feedback to each other. This type of student learning encourages a supportive classroom environment, while still allowing students to showcase their learning safely, knowing mistakes are okay and part of the process.

Phew! That was a lot of information! Good work for pushing through and keeping your mind open to new and exciting suggestions to implement in your classroom. The next portion of a Leveled-Up Lesson Plan is optional and may not be necessary in every single lesson; however, it is one of my favorite parts of any lesson it is incorporated in. I also believe it strengthens the classroom environment to teach students to work together, problem-solve, and appreciate the unique talents their classmates possess. So, with that, let's move on to "Multiplayer Mode: Collaborative Practice in Your Lessons."

CHAPTER 6

Multiplayer Mode Collaborative Practice in Your Lessons

When substituting in classrooms, I noticed students today can struggle with communicating with their peers. With the constant distraction of screens, talking with others has been a skill that is not as prominent as it should be. This seemed like a problem because having the ability to work together and problem solve is necessary in real-life situations. It got me thinking, "How can I get students working collaboratively but still learning and having fun?" This was a real dilemma I thought about on a daily basis. I saw a problem and wanted to find a solution.

Then, one day, I had a lightbulb moment. While watching my girls do some art projects together, I saw them giggling and laughing while also creating a beautiful work of art. I started to wonder if there was a way to combine this type of experience with other subjects like math. A few days later, I was at a friend's house and noticed she had a large coloring poster, the size of her kitchen table, laid out for her children to color. Again, I thought, this would be a cool concept to pair with lessons in the classroom.

Often, this is how my best ideas come to me. I have a problem, and as I think of solutions, I can piece ideas together based on my experiences from my daily life or things I see "out in the wild." The product that was born was my Collaborative Canvas Posters. I wanted something where students were working together, being creative, and reviewing standards and concepts taught by their teachers.

The Collaborative Canvas Posters are more than just a visual aid; they are an immersive, hands-on experience that brings students together to reinforce and review key concepts in a dynamic and engaging way. The posters are large, 36×24 in. and are meant to be a central focus on a bulletin board or in the hallway when completed. Each poster is packed with questions that challenge students to think critically and apply their knowledge. The interactive paper pieces, such as fraction wheels, folded paper books with hidden answers, and pockets holding vocabulary cards add a tactile element to the learning process. These paper pieces not only make the posters visually appealing but also provide a variety of ways for students to interact with the content.

The collaborative nature of this project is key to its success. By grouping students in small teams of three to four, you create a supportive environment where they can work through the problems together. This group setting allows students to share ideas, discuss solutions, and help each other understand difficult concepts without the pressure of working alone. The collaborative approach reduces the likelihood of students feeling overwhelmed and instead fosters a sense of confidence as they realize they can tackle the project as a team.

I also noticed, when I introduced these posters to students, they were excited to work on a project together. The opportunity to team up, talk openly, and engage with material in a hands-on way transformed the learning experience. Instead of silently struggling through worksheets or finishing tasks quickly and becoming bored, students were actively engaged, each with a specific role to play in completing the poster. This sense of purpose definitely kept them focused and motivated throughout the lesson.

The final step of the project, where students present their completed posters, added another layer of value to this collaborative project. Their presentations of their work not only reinforced the material but also gave students a sense of pride and accomplishment. Students saw the results of their teamwork and understood the importance of collaboration and working together.

After creating these posters and watching them in action, I was even more convinced that collaboration should be a key component in any classroom. Every single lesson doesn't need a collaborative piece or need to be as in-depth as the Collaborative Canvas Posters. However, sprinkling in collaborative opportunities in different lessons throughout the week is a quick way to build community and strengthen your student's understanding of concepts being taught.

WHAT IS COLLABORATION IN THE CLASSROOM?

Before we go much further, let's go over what collaboration in the classroom is and what it looks like. Collaboration in a classroom setting would mean students are actively engaged with one another to achieve shared objectives, exchange ideas, and collectively solve problems. Students aren't merely working side-by-side but are actively participating with one another on a group task. Since students are working together, they are required to communicate effectively, listen to different perspectives, and learn from one another's strengths. Social interaction is a huge part of collaboration where students can share their unique ideas in a comfortable setting rather than just receive information passively from the teacher.

In a collaborative setting, students all bring their unique backgrounds and experiences to the table, which enriches the process for everyone. This collective effort allows for deeper understanding of the topic and helps students solidify their own understanding of what they are learning. Collaboration also often leads to the development of higher-order thinking skills, such as analysis and evaluation, because students engage critically with the content and with each other's ideas. Students also learn that it is important to listen to all ideas because it is often a great idea that is born after all shared ideas are combined and thought through.

When implementing collaborative projects into your classroom, it is essential to teach and incorporate several key principles to form the foundation for effective teamwork. These principles should not only guide students as they interact but also ensure the collaborative projects are meaningful and productive. Let's go over the key principles you should implement:

- **Effective communication**: Communication is the cornerstone of any successful collaboration. In a classroom. This would look like students expressing themselves clearly while their peers listen respectfully and actively. When you are effectively communicating, you are not only speaking but also understanding and listening to what others say. This could involve agreeing (or politely disagreeing) with what is shared, asking thoughtful questions, or even giving kind and constructive feedback.

- **Cooperation and teamwork**: This principle goes beyond just working side-by-side; it involves weaving thoughts and skills together as a group. Cooperation requires a willingness to compromise, negotiate, and sometimes even adapt personal preferences for the benefit of the group as a whole. Adapting can be the hardest concept to teach students because they usually want to do things their own way, but learning to adapt and be flexible is a technique that can be carried with them throughout their entire lives. Working as a team should also help students understand their role in the group and give them a sense of accountability and commitment to the project. Cooperating and sharing teamwork means everyone is involved in the end goal, and the work is shared and balanced with all involved.

- **Respect for diverse perspectives**: Within your classroom, all students bring their own diverse thoughts, opinions, and experiences. While learning content and standards is important so is understanding the diversity of others. Students should learn not to just accept differences but celebrate them, too. Collaborative work can help students learn the value of diversity as they problem solve and make decisions together. By encouraging students to engage with others and look at different points of view, you are helping them develop critical thinking skills that they can carry with them into their adult lives and careers.

- **Shared responsibility**: Have you ever been part of a "group project" that you ended up completing all by yourself? I have, and it is not fun! Successful collaboration comes from a collective effort from all members of the group. Whether you assign different tasks or roles to students or hold student's accountable for the work they contribute, it is important that during collaborative exercises all students are responsible to hold up their end of the project. Emphasizing shared responsibility can also help students learn leadership skills as they guide each other through the project.

By incorporating these principles into your lessons and collaborative activities, you create a classroom culture that values teamwork, respects diversity, and emphasizes the importance of communication and responsibility.

WHY COLLABORATION IS IMPORTANT IN THE CLASSROOM

Imagine a group of fourth-grade students working around a table trying to figure out how to build the tallest tower while only being given uncooked spaghetti and marshmallows. At first, they struggle to communicate and figure out a plan. Everyone is talking over each other, and it seems the endeavor might fail. All the children are trying to build their own tower and believes their idea is superior to others. Soon, one child begins to take charge and listens to what others have to say. The students begin to realize that combining their ideas may be the best way to build the tallest tower. Students figure out that working together and combining skills helps them not only reach new heights with their tower, but with their accomplishments, too. This simple activity helped teach students that collaboration not only makes learning fun but also teaches students that they are stronger together.

Collaboration is important in any classroom because it helps develop critical skills, promotes deeper learning, prepares students for the future, and fosters a positive classroom environment. When writing your lesson plans, try to include collaboration whenever you can, to expand these areas for your students. It may not make sense for every lesson to include collaboration, but when it does, it definitely has its bonus points!

Critical abilities students can learn from collaboration include communication skills, problem-solving skills, and empathy, which are essential both in and out of school. It is important to note that while not every lesson may lend itself naturally to collaboration, the lessons that do can offer tremendous benefits. Collaborative material encourages students to engage more deeply with the material, as they work together to share ideas, solve problems, and complete tasks. In fact, one of the prime benefits of collaboration is the development of communication skills. When students collaborate, they must express their thoughts clearly, listen to other perspectives, and articulate their reasonings. These are skills that take years to learn and a lifetime to master. Why not offer as many opportunities in the classroom to practice them?

In today's interconnected world, collaboration is more important than ever in almost any career a student chooses. Even people who have the opportunity to work from home need to learn to collaborate online! And that is a skill in and of itself. A student may choose a career path like healthcare, education, finance, or sales among an endless options of careers out there, and the ability to collaborate will become one of their most valuable assets because, oftentimes, our best ideas become our greatest achievements as we take perspectives from others.

Having projects that incorporate STEM are a great way to mimic real-world teamwork scenarios. Each group member might take a different role in the project, such as researcher, designer, or presenter. However, all the students need to work together to complete the final end result to see the project succeed. These types of activities mirror the type of collaboration required in professional settings and can help prepare students for the future.

Collaboration can also help create a positive and inclusive classroom environment because it encourages students to work together, respect each other's perspectives, and cultivate community. As students work together they will cultivate inclusion. Instead of competing with one another, students are cooperating and coming together. The pressure to outperform their peers is taken off of the students and instead is replaced with shared responsibility and mutual success.

HOW TO IMPLEMENT COLLABORATION IN LESSON PLANS

As a teacher, you know your students best. You understand when you should and how often you should create experiences where students can work with their peers either in pairs or groups. Choosing the best subjects or times of day to implement collaborative work is really up to you! However, it can be quite easy to integrate collaboration into various subjects and lessons with purposeful planning. Let's discuss some effectives ways to incorporate collaboration into your lesson plans.

■ **Group projects**: Now don't roll your eyes. Group projects don't have to be scary or something to shy away from. We have all been part of that "one group," where you worked "as a team," but really you ended up doing every aspect of the assignment. Sure, when rushed and not monitored correctly by the teacher, group work can be frustrating. However, if students are assigned roles and expectations are set, group work can be a positive way to incorporate collaborations. When assigning group projects, I suggest grading all students individually based on their role in the group and not the group as a whole project only. This way, the individual student can still succeed but doesn't feel the weight and responsibility of the entire task.

For example, during a science lesson, your students might be learning about ecosystems. Each group member can be responsible for a specific aspect of the project like plant life, animal life, climate, and food sources. All members would be in charge of researching their aspect of the project, and then all members could come together to create the presentation in a meaningful way.

■ **Collaborative learning stations**: As mentioned, when I was teaching sixth grade in an elementary school, I loved doing learning stations during language arts. I simply called them *language arts centers*. Centers can be really diverse. Whether you want them to be centers for independent practice or as a way for students to collaborate, learning stations are a flexible way to allow students to collaborate together. I liked that my students could rotate through different centers, where some they'd do independently, while in other centers they were required to work with a partner or group. Having at least one center that required a collaborative component gave us a chance *daily* to have students collaborate and for me to work with students who needed extra support. I found it to be a win-win!

Collaborative learning stations are an effective way to integrate collaboration into your lesson on a daily basis, without having to take up too much time out of your day. By carefully organizing stations and creating clear expectations, students can stay on task and accomplish meaningful work to help them master essential standards.

- **Think-pair-share**: One of the simplest strategies when fostering collaboration in your classroom is to use Think-Pair-Share. Whether reviewing before a test, learning a new concept, or asking thoughtful questions to your students, this collaborative strategy can work with almost any lesson. First, ask a question to your students: any question! It could be during a math lesson, writing activity, or while reading a story for example. Then have your students think about their answer individually. They can just think about it or even write down their own thoughts. Next, have students pair together and share their answers with a classmate. Finally, have a few students share their answers and thoughts with the whole class.

- **Jigsaw method**: Like the name suggests, with this collaborative method, student groups each take one piece of the puzzle, or lesson, and are responsible for teaching it to the whole class. For example, during history lessons about the American Revolution, different groups would be assigned different events that led up to the American Revolution. Then the groups would learn about their specific topic, create a presentation, and later teach the whole class what they learned.

- **Digital tools for collaboration**: Using technology in the classroom is one of my favorite ways to support collaboration. There are SO MANY tools, it can be overwhelming. So, I will give you a list of some of my favorite, tried and true digital tools for collaboration.

  o *PowerPoint*: At its most basic form, PowerPoint would be just perceived as a presentation tool. However, it is a great resource to get students working together. Teachers can assign students to work together on different slides, giving responsibility to different members of the group. Students can research a topic and present it together. PowerPoint also has a comment feature. This allows students to leave notes for each other as they collaborate, helping them refine their project together.

  o *Google Docs*: Google Docs is probably one of the most versatile and widely used collaborative tools in education, and it is free! It gives students the perfect platform to work together on written assignments and projects. Whether they are editing stories or essays, creating outlines together, writing research papers together, or revising documents, they can do it together seamlessly. Google Docs gives teachers the power to assign writing tasks where students collaboratively research together, peer-edit each other's work, or divide sections of a document to tackle individually. Additionally, Google Docs has commenting and suggesting features to allow students to leave feedback. Also, the revision history feature lets students track changes made by any group member, ensuring everything is done correctly and fairly between members. With Google Docs, students don't even need to be in the same classroom or on the same computer. They can be working from different locations but still collaborating together.

o *Google Slides*: Much like PowerPoint, Google Slides is often thought of just as a presentation tool. However, when thinking of collaboration, I might suggest that Google Slides is actually more powerful than PowerPoint. Since, like Google Docs, students can work on the same presentation, but from different computers and locations. While it doesn't have as robust of features as PowerPoint, it has enough to make it work for students in a classroom. Each student can work on different slides within the same presentation, at different times, all while real-time updates are being made. So, whether students are working in class together, or at their own homes on homework assignments, Google Slides makes collaboration virtually flawless. Google Slides also easily allows for the use of elements like animations or videos embedded in the presentations. This can add an extra depth into the student's group presentation.

o *Canva*: Hands down, my very favorite online tool in education to date. Not only is it completely free for teachers to use in their classrooms, but it also offers a lot of what PowerPoint, Google Docs, and Google Slides can, plus so much more! Canva is an amazing tool when having students create creative projects together. Whether they are creating videos, posters, graphics, presentations, infographics, writing papers, comic strips, gifs, or digital games, Canva's powerful design features makes it user friendly and easy to figure out for students. Teachers can assign group projects where students collaborate on a Canva design together, whether they are creating a visual representation of a historical event, designing a class newsletter, or developing promotional materials for a mock business project, Canva allows for ease of use in all of these scenarios. Canva is one tool you should not pass up as a teacher, not just for your own use, but to have students use as well.

Now that you have some practical ideas for implementing collaboration into your lessons, let's dive deeper into the types of projects that can enhance both learning and engagement in your classroom. As mentioned before, teaching should strike a balance between being fun and educational. However, it's important to remember that every activity, lesson, or project should serve a clear purpose. Simply filling time or completing tasks to check them off a list is not effective teaching. Instead, your activities should be intentional, thoughtfully designed to meet specific learning objectives and help students grow. In the next section, we'll explore a variety of activities and projects that not only promote collaboration but also add real value to your students' learning experience. These projects will be engaging, purposeful and aligned with your educational goals, ensuring that your students gain valuable skills while enjoying the learning process.

COLLABORATIVE ACTIVITIES AND PROJECTS

As we have been discussing, collaboration is an important part of modern education today because it helps students build skills like communication, teamwork, and problem-solving skills. It is more important than ever to create opportunities where students can work together, share ideas, and learn from one another. Collaborative activities not only make learning more engaging, but they also help students build connections with peers and strengthen their understanding of different concepts as they take on responsibility toward group success.

It's time to level up your lesson plans with collaborative activities. Let's go over, in more detail, specific activities and projects you can implement in your classroom that promote collaboration:

- **Group story writing**: With this, students collaborate on a story together. Students begin with a story starter or journal prompt. Then, each student adds a sentence or paragraph to the writing, building on what the previous students have written. This is a great way to show creativity and build teamwork. Students will also need to connect their ideas so the story flows well, this way allowing students to communicate with each other.
  - To implement this, divide students into groups. Give each group a topic or opening sentence. All students will then take turns adding to their story either verbally or in writing, until the story is complete. Add extra layers of difficulty by requiring a certain number of sentences or paragraphs.
- **Collaborative posters**: Giant posters that students work on together, like my Collaborative Canvas Posters, are an excellent way to not only review content but share ideas and solve problems together. Students love creating and solving the problems together, lessening the stress of completing an assignment individually.
  - To implement collaborative posters, divide students into groups of three to four. Provide the materials needed, like the poster, markers, scissors, and glue. Allow students to work on their posters together and then have groups present their posters to the class when finished.
- **STEM challenges**: STEM, which stands for Science, Technology, Engineering, and Math, challenges engage students in hands-on activities that require them to apply concepts from multiple subjects to solve real-world problems. STEM challenges often involve designing and building structures, conducting experiments, or solving engineering puzzles with limited resources. Through their collaboration, students learn to communicate their ideas while testing and refining their strategies.
  - To implement a STEM challenge, first define your challenge. Make sure it aligns with objectives being taught in your classroom.

A good STEM challenge has clear goals and a specific framework. For instance, you might have students build the tallest tower by using only paper and tape. The challenge should require trial and error. Next set the guidelines. Providing a rubric helps students see what their end goal should look like. Then you will split students into groups and allow them to plan and brainstorm their solutions to the challenge together. Once their planning is done, they will begin building, testing, and refining their strategies. When the challenge is complete, have students reflect on the process and consider what they would do the same and what they would change about their experience.

- **Peer teaching**: This is a powerful collaboration strategy because students take on the role of teacher, teaching concepts or skills to their own classmates. Sometimes, a student explains it best in "kid talk" to a student who just can't seem to grasp the concept from the teacher. This method promotes active learning and encourages the students to take responsibility for their learning. It also helps students who are naturally leaders use their leadership skills in the classroom. The process of teaching a concept requires a deeper understanding of the standard, which will help solidify the concept for the student teaching it.
  - This type of collaboration can be done several different ways. You can have students informally explaining topics to other students or have a student presenting on a specific topic in a very formal and structured setting. The key, however, is to ensure the students have a sufficient understanding of the material so it can be taught effectively.
- **Reader's theater**: One of my favorite activities during literacy block was to incorporate a reader's theater. This involves giving students a script (the length depends on what type of script you choose) and having students take different parts. Then students practice reading their parts with emotion, character voices, and emphasis. This helps students practice fluency and comprehension while working as a team to bring a story together.
  - To implement, break your students into several groups. Give each group a different Reader's Theater script. After allowing students

to practice their scripts together and have them read their scripts aloud to the class. It may even be fun to allow students another day to practice and add movements to their reader's theater, if time allows.

- **Escape rooms**: While there is an entire chapter dedicated to escape rooms in this book, I did want to mention it here during the collaboration section because escape rooms in the classroom are a wonderful way to get students moving, working together, and using critical thinking skills. In fact, escape rooms may be my favorite way to encourage collaboration. They can take some prep, so they are not activities to be used every day but might be used for end-of-unit reviews or as a special day in the classroom. Escape rooms can literally be used for *any* subject and topic. They are very versatile. Typically, the teacher will introduce a scenario or story, such as being trapped in a lab or lost in a jungle. Students must solve clues to problems to escape the situation.
  - To carry out your escape room, you will need to do a bit of planning by picking a theme and then designing puzzles, challenges, and clues that go along with the theme. Think of it like a scavenger hunt but with questions that are standard-based interwoven throughout the experience, with secret decoders and puzzles sprinkled in. Once you have your game, you will split your students into groups. They will be given a time limit and must find and correctly complete all the tasks before time runs out to escape. If this seems like a brief explanation, it is. So, we will go more in depth in Chapter 10 about using escape rooms to level up your lesson plans and the different types you can implement.
- **Classroom debates**: Whether you are discussing how to defend an argument when writing an essay or learning about different historical events, debates can be a great way for students to practice critical thinking as they defend their opinions as well as listening as they take in what other students have to say. Not to mention, it is a great exercise in speaking publicly in front of groups.
  - Put this collaborative strategy into action by dividing students into pairs or groups. Give each group of students a topic to debate. Allow enough time for each team to collaborate on their arguments,

research their positions, and prepare for the debate whether that includes creating presentations or just practicing speaking their parts aloud. Students can then take turns presenting their arguments and responding to their opponents' points.

- **Project-based learning**: Project-based learning (PBL) is a type of lesson or set of activities that requires students to engage in authentic inquiry and hands-on learning as they dive deeply into a topic over a sustained period of time rather than completing several different, isolated assignments. Students are often solving problems in real-world scenarios, such as being given a budget and job assignment and planning out their monthly expenses. They might budget for groceries, rent, and extracurricular activities.

  - To implement PBL activities, assign projects that relate to the unit or students you are currently teaching. For instance, you may be teaching about area and perimeter, so the students will be designing a new playground for the school. The students would collaborate and brainstorm what to include, design their models, and present their ideas to the class. They may have a budget for cost, a map for the size of the equipment, and the space it will take up, as well as plans for how it will be used.

- **Collaborative mind maps**: These are interactive and visual tools that allow students to work together and brainstorm and organize their ideas. A mind map is essentially a diagram that represents connections between different concepts with a central idea at the core. Branches lead to related ideas, topics, or subtopics. When students collaborate on a mind map, they build on each other's ideas, identity connections, and develop a deeper understanding of the subject matter. Mind maps are also a great way to help students visualize their thinking as they put it on paper. Mind maps could be used in writing, reading, science, and history topics really well as you compare different events and topics.

  - Mind maps are rather easy to facilitate in your classroom. Begin by selecting a topic that covers an objective you are teaching. For example, have students analyze characters in a book they are reading. After you group students together, have them set up their mind map. It could be done on paper or on sites like Canva. Students would put their topic (like a character from their reading) in the center. Then they will create branches of different subtopics and connect them with other ideas and topics using lines and arrows. When groups are finished, they can present their mind maps to the class.

- **Partner reading**: A great way to encourage more reading in your classroom, practice fluency, and get students working together is to do partner reading. This is as simple as it sounds: students partner together and take turns reading passages together. Whether it is a passage assigned from the teacher, pages from a book they are reading, or their own writing students are reading, partner reading helps students develop all kinds of skills.
  - To implement this strategy, simply pair students together to read. Students don't need to be on the same reading levels to be partners. In fact, it might help to have varied levels together so students can model reading for each other and give each other feedback.

By incorporating collaboration into your classroom, you build a sense of community and empower your students to take ownership of their learning. When students work together, they develop essential life skills such as communication, problem solving, and adaptability, which will serve them well beyond the classroom walls. As a teacher, when you integrate collaborative activities and projects, as you tie them to standards, you will begin to notice your students excited about learning and more interested in their school experience. Emphasizing collaboration in the classroom is not just a teaching strategy; it's a vital investment in our students' future success.

CHAPTER 7

Assessment: The Lesson Plan Victory Lap

Does anyone truly enjoy assessments, whether giving them or taking them? While they are an essential part of education, allowing teachers to evaluate where students stand, assess whether the material is being retained, and help plan for future lessons, they often carry a heavy weight. Both teachers and students can find assessments stressful, not because they have to be but because of the pressure associated with them.

I remember having 32 students in my classroom, all on varying levels, yet being expected to get every one of them to pass the state tests at grade level. It was a goal everyone in education knew was impossible; there was no way every student would be at the same level. Still, I pushed myself beyond the limits, working tirelessly, with most of my students doing the same. Despite our efforts, achieving 100 percent success at grade level was simply unrealistic.

The pressure to meet this unattainable standard weighed heavily on me. It wasn't just the fear of failing a test; it was the fear of letting everyone down, meaning my students, their parents, my principal, and the school. I carried this burden, given to me by the state legislators, and didn't recognize the individual growth and progress my students were making like I should have. My anxiety stemmed from focusing on that external benchmark instead of celebrating the real success happening in my classroom: My students were learning, improving, and moving forward. That should have been the real victory.

After a couple years of this mentality, I switched gears. I made goals for growth for each individual student. We spoke about these goals, we wrote about them, and we aimed to achieve our personal bests. Assessing students should be done on an individual level and with the understanding that no two students are the same. Learning strategies differ, and so do test-taking skills. Students are not their tests; however, assessments should be used to gauge progress and celebrate achievements.

The last portion to plan for your lesson plan should be the assessment. Each lesson will not have a big unit test or quiz because there are many different ways and methods for assessing students. Before we discuss how to level up your assessments, we need to define and distinguish formative and summative assessment, as well as cover the purpose of assessing students.

PURPOSE OF ASSESSMENTS

Assessment is important in education because it helps us monitor student progress. It also gives a purpose to our teaching and holds both the teacher and student accountable. Assessments should not limit our students but have a purpose to serve their greater good overall.

I remember starting one school year, and as an entire faculty, we made a goal to guide us in improving student reading scores across the entire school in every grade level. The principal had a giant chart in her office with each grade, teacher, students, and where the students were on their reading level. Based on their level, it was determined how much intervention was needed for that student. Plans were put into place to help these students make progress. However, to monitor and check for progress, we had to perform reading tests. Each test was only one minute long, and the students read a passage as we counted words for accuracy and fluency and then asked comprehension questions after. Some students were tested every couple days, while others just once a week or once every other week.

I will not sugarcoat this experience. It was a lot of work, but we saw so much growth and progress for our students! The testing was not high stakes. It was familiar and something the students understood was needed to meet progress goals. Students would record their scores in a booklet and watch their numbers get better and better. Each student had a goal for progress, and it was a group effort to get them there.

This strategy worked well, and I want to applaud the principal and all the teachers involved in this task. It was no easy accomplishment, but by the end of the year, we were all proud of meeting goals and helping students meet their potential.

Assessment has a place in all classrooms. Not every lesson needs a summative chapter test. However, formative and summative assessment, intermixed within the classroom, can help guide teachers in understanding what to teach, when, and for how long.

FORMATIVE ASSESSMENTS

Most lessons will include formative assessments. Formative assessments are low stakes, meaning they are used to monitor student learning and progress. It is not a final evaluation or formal test. Formative assessments, however, do play a crucial role for teachers because they help monitor student progress on a regular basis. This type of assessment is meant to provide ongoing feedback for students but also help teachers adjust their daily lesson plans as needed based on the needs of their students. Formative assessments give teachers a path to follow.

Sometimes, teachers focus on getting to the finish line. They teach and move on. However, if students are not grasping a concept, it is okay to slow down and reteach standards. In fact, slowing down can actually help you speed up the learning process in the long run because you are catching misconceptions early and fixing any misunderstandings. This is why it is important to put an emphasis on formative assessment so you can understand where your students are in their learning.

All teachers have had the humbling experience of passing out a quiz, test, or project only for it to be turned in and you are surprised by the results, and they're not good. You thought your lessons were hitting the mark, but your test results say otherwise. This can be a discouraging moment for a teacher. One way to combat this is with simple formative assessments. Yes, they should be simple! These types of assessments should not be stressful for you or the student, and they should not carry a lot of weight in terms of grades, if any. Informative assessment is meant to provide immediate feedback, keep students engaged, and help with differentiated learning when necessary.

Asking simple questions like, "Give me a thumbs up or thumbs down if you understand this concept?" is a great way to quickly gauge where students are in your lesson. Exit tickets are another tool that can help you as a teacher check for understanding. An exit ticket is a slip of paper with two to four questions on it that relate to the subject being taught. They are to be handed out at the end of a lesson. Students can quickly fill out their exit ticket and give it to the teacher. Because it is not a surprise quiz or a test with tons of questions, a teacher can easily look over the exit slips and see where their students are at in terms of understanding the current standard being taught. Formative assessment often offers more real time feedback and makes it the perfect tool for teachers to help them assess and plan for their daily lessons.

Let's level up your formative assessment strategies and get your lesson planning rounded off with quality student evaluations. Here are 30 fun and engaging ways to perform formative assessments in your classroom:

1. **Emoji assessment**: Students love emojis! Create four to five different emoji cards. A smiley could represent complete understanding, a winky face could mean a student mostly understands the topic, and all the way to a confused emoji, meaning the student needs more help or has questions. Laminate the emoji assessment cards and give each student a set. Then, during or after a lesson, have students pull out their emoji assessment cards. They are to raise the card that best matches how they are feeling about the topic.

2. **Be the illustrator**: After reading a passage of text, have students illustrate what was read. This is a great way to see if students are comprehending and visualizing what they are reading. It is also a unique approach to having students summarize what they've read.

3. **Text message summary**: When text messaging was first coming around, there was a character limit for each text. Give students a slip of paper with a speech bubble, and tell them to summarize what they learned in 140 characters or fewer. Each letter and punctuation mark counts as a character.

4. **Bull's eye**: Have a target poster hanging in your classroom. Once the lesson is complete, give each student a sticky note. They are to write their name and place the sticky note on the target to match their understanding. So, if they are confident in their understanding of the lesson, their sticky note would go on the bull's-eye.

5. **Sentence, phrase, word**: When your lesson is complete, students will write a sentence to summarize their learning. Then they will underline the most important phrase in the sentence that explains the lesson. Finally, they will circle the most important word.

6. **Learning web**: This would be similar to a mind map. Students are creating a web of understanding. At the center of the web, they will write what the lesson was about and then write branches off of the web with examples, samples, or definitions that support what is in the center of the web.

7. **Whiteboards**: This is one I used *all* the time. Students always loved writing on their own personal whiteboard. I would give them a marker, small eraser, and personal-sized whiteboard to keep at their desk. Then, during math for example, I would post questions on the board and allow students to show their work and solve the question on their whiteboard. Afterward, I would say, "Show your board in 3. . .2. . .1. . .," and students would hold up their answers. I could quickly scan to see who got it correct and see the work they did to come to their answer.

8. **Exit slips**: Mentioned earlier, these are half or quarter sheets of paper with two to four questions on them. The questions relate to the topic being taught. At the end of the lesson, before students can exit the classroom, they must hand in their slip of paper with their answers. This gives the teacher a quick way to gauge assessment and understanding.

9. **Partner interviews**: This is a great formative assessment that can also be collaborative! Students will partner up and ask each other three questions about the lesson. As they ask each other questions, the teacher can walk around and listen to responses to check for understanding.

10. **Four corners**: This would be similar to a multiple-choice quiz but letting students be active. Label each corner in your classroom A, B,

C, and D. Then ask a question that relates to the topic being taught and give four answer choices. Students will then walk to the corner that matches their answer.

11. **1, 2, 3, 4**: Similar to Four corners, but this formative assessment strategy is done with students at their desk. Instead of walking to a corner, they will hold up a finger for their answer. So, you will ask a multiple-choice question and give four answer choices. Students will hold up 1, 2, 3, or 4 fingers for their answer.

12. **Red light/green light**: Create some cards that are red on one side and green on the other. I suggest laminating two pieces of construction paper together, one green and one red. Then cut the paper into quarters. Give each student their one red light/green light. During lessons, as you are teaching, stop and ask students how they are feeling about what they are learning. A green indicates they are good, while red will let you know they still have questions or need help.

13. **Comic strips**: Instead of students summarizing what they have learned or read in a paragraph, have them do it by creating a comic strip! Pass out a blank comic board. Instruct students to fill in each box and create a comic to showcase what they learned.

14. **Dear future student**: Have students write a quick letter or email about a lesson they just learned to a student coming to your class next year. They can write and explain about what the topic was and things the future student can look out for that might be a bit tricky.

15. **Spot the rerror**: While teaching a specific objective, during the lesson, occasionally pause and say, "Spot the error!" Write an example question on the board with one intentional mistake. Have students find the error and tell it to a partner.

16. **Two truths and a lie**: This could be done from the point of view of the teacher or student. After a lesson, write three statements on the board that relate to the lesson just taught. One of them being a lie. Have students pick out the lie and write their answer on a slip of paper. Additionally, you could also have students write their own three statements with one being false. Students can trade their two truths and a lie papers with a partner.

17. **Student-made quiz**: Instead of writing a quiz yourself, have the students do it! At the end of the lesson, have students write one question about what was taught. Gather the questions and use three to four of them for your class. Have students write their answers on a sheet of paper, give thumbs up or down, use white boards, or just shout out answers.

18. **Venn diagram**: Graphic organizers are a great way to check for comprehension. Using a Venn diagram is a very basic graphic organizer. It helps to visually display the relationship between two different sets of items, concepts, or ideas by showing their similarities and differences through overlapping circles. Use Venn diagrams to compare historical figures or events, math strategies, characters or settings in a story, animal habitats, science concepts, and more!

19. **Social post**: It is no secret that social media is a part of our lives. Whether students have social media or not, they are aware of what it is. Hand students a slip of paper with a post template. They can draw a picture to illustrate what they learned from the lesson and write a short caption for the photo, even including relevant hashtags if desired!

20. **What matters most**: Lessons are usually going to be jam-packed with good information. However, there is always one idea or thought that is the *most* important. For this formative assessment strategy, simply have students write a one-sentence summary of what they think mattered most in the lesson they just learned.

21. **Popsicle sticks**: As a way to assess understanding throughout a lesson and to get more than the regular hands in the air answering questions, put student names on popsicle sticks. Place the sticks in a cup near the front of the classroom. As you ask questions throughout your teaching, pull a stick and read the name. That student will be asked to answer the question first.

22. **Keep the questions going**: Ask a question for understanding to one student; then the student who answered your question turns to another student and asks another question based on the lesson. Do this with as many students as you would like. For example, say, "We are going to keep the questions going for five students. . .10 students," etc.

23. **30-second news report**: Students love this one! Turn your lessons into breaking news segments. After you are finished teaching a standard, give students 30 seconds to recap it as a news story to a partner. To elevate the fun, try to occasionally have students record their news segments.

24. **Poll them**: Use a bit of technology and do an anonymous class poll. There are a ton of free websites that allow for classroom polling. Most require some sort of technology whether students are holding up QR codes or using computers to insert answers. Whatever the case, create polls to check for understanding after a lesson.

25. **SOS summary**: In this formative strategy the first S stands for "Statement," the O stands for "Opinion," and the last S stands for "Support." Upon lesson completion, a teacher will give a statement, and students will write their opinion with a fact or example to support their opinion.

26. **Postcards**: Create some blank postcards by simply cutting paper into fourths. On one side, students illustrate what was learned for the day. On the back, students will write a short letter to someone, whether a character from a book you are reading, a historical figure from the lesson that was taught, or someone else, describing what was learned.

27. **Roses and thorns**: Students write two things they understood or liked about the topic (roses) and one question or thing they didn't understand (thorn).

28. **Self-assessment**: Have students reflect on their own learning and write two to three sentences explaining how they feel about the lesson. Consider adding a smiley, straight face, and sad emoji that students circle to match their self-assessment. Then they can describe why they circled the emoji that they did.

29. **Roll the die**: Apply one statement to each number like 1 is "I learned today that. . .," 2 is "I am still confused about. . .," 3 is "Something important from today's lesson was. . .," 4 is "I am confident about this from the lesson. . .," 5 is "I have one question about. . .," and 6 is "One fact from the lesson was. . . ." Roll a die for the class and have everyone answer.

30. **Always, sometimes, never**: Ask a question and students must respond with that it happens always, sometimes, or never.

Check out the formative assessment templates included with this book! Simply scan this QR code or type the link in your browser to get the bonus material.

teresakwant.com/bonus-material/
Password: levelup

SUMMATIVE ASSESSMENTS

One of the longest tests I personally ever took was in college. It was my Praxis 2 test to graduate school and become a certified teacher. I studied hard for this and felt prepared. What I did not study for was the fact that it would take four hours. By the end of the test, I remember finishing an essay question and forgetting how to properly spell "their." It was a bit embarrassing because I knew how to spell it, but my brain was fried. I had sat in front of a computer for four hours. There was no spell-check, so I just wrote it *their* and then later as *thier*. Better to have it spelled right in at least one place! While I understand the need for taking the test and having qualified professionals, not all tests will accurately judge someone's intellectual ability. Yes, I passed with flying colors. Yes, I am sure some person correcting the test laughed wondering why I couldn't spell that word, but in the end, I got the score I deserved and became a teacher. I guess they were able to overlook one misspelling, with all the other words being spelled correctly.

All this to say, summative assessments are a needed part of education in measuring progress and ability, but they don't always show us the whole picture of students or highlight all of their strengths. There is no way one test that is done with paper and pencil (or on a computer) can show us all the skills and talents our students possess. So, yes, test your students. Challenge them to be their best intellectual selves, but let us also remember that not all skills and talents can be measured with a unit test or even a standardized test.

Summative assessments are needed to help us measure a student's understanding, knowledge, and skills at the end of a unit, term, or even academic year. Although summative assessments do not need to be done on a scantron sheet (okay, I dated myself there) or strictly done as multiple-choice questions mixed with short-answer questions. While these types of assessments can be effective, sometimes it is good to think outside the box and add a bit of fun *and* learning.

Remember, not every test will measure skills of a student accurately, because not every student learns the same. So, it might be nice to mix up your testing occasionally. Assessing students helps teachers learn how to teach their students because after an assessment, you may determine you need to change things up! Summative assessment also helps teachers and schools determine which programs are working and helping their students meet learning goals.

One major difference between a formative assessment and summative assessment is that summative assessments give a final overview of an entire unit of study. It is usually weighted more in terms of grades. So, for students and teachers, summative assessments require more buy-in or responsibility on everyone's part.

Another difference with summative assessments is the timing. These tests come at the end of the unit, or even end of the year. They are used to give final grades or scores as a final indicator of the concepts learned. They are definitely high stakes in comparison to formative assessments.

One last difference between formative and summative assessment is the purpose. Formative assessment is meant to guide the learning process, while summative evaluates that learning has taken place. This is a key difference and is why the assessing may look and feel different when giving a summative versus a formative assessment. Also, formative assessment often gives immediate feedback to students so they can shape their thinking, while summative assessment provides the final grade or evaluation of the learning.

While many will argue unit tests are a necessary part of education, occasionally, it is okay to mix up the way we evaluate students. Summative assessments don't always need to be standard because not all students fit a standard model. So, I would like to share 20 different ideas you can use when assessing students in a summative evaluation that does not require a unit or chapter test.

Think of these summative assessment examples as culminating projects where students apply what they've learned. Instead of a traditional test, students will create a final product that demonstrates their understanding of the entire unit or chapter of study. Their work will be evaluated using a rubric or grading scale, ensuring a comprehensive assessment of their knowledge and skills in a meaningful, hands-on way.

1. **Infographic**: An infographic is a visual representation of information. It can mix together text, data, timelines, and pictures to explain complex ideas. Students can use programs like Canva or PowerPoint to create digital infographics. Or they can use giant poster boards, with markers, and make paper-based infographics.

2. **Presentation slides**: Creating slides is a simple and creative way for students to showcase what they have learned. Whether they use Google Slides, Canva, PowerPoint, or another program, they can add text, images, and animations to create a presentation to show the class.

3. **Brochure**: Students can brainstorm and outline a brochure or pamphlet that thoroughly explains the topic they have learned. Once the outline is complete and information has been gathered, they can create a brochure by folding a paper in thirds or do it digitally. Students can include text and visuals to really make their brochures stand out!

4. **Wanted poster**: This is a fun idea to use for a book report or history report! However, it could be used for science as well. Think of things that could be wanted, like a scientific element, a specific animal, or a type of math algorithm. Students then create a catchy title for their poster. Again, this could be done with a traditional poster board or digitally. Next, students write a description of the item/person/thing that is wanted and list the "crimes" or "contributions"

this person or concept has made. Also, a picture of the wanted person, thing, or idea should be included. If desired, students can also write a reward for the capture of their wanted person or concept.

5. **Diorama**: A diorama is a great way for students to showcase specific scenes, elements or figures of a unit that has been taught. One way to level it up even more is to have students also write an essay to go with their project. Have students use a shoebox and other materials, such as construction paper, play dough, clay, and toy figurines, to build their scene. Consider showcasing all the dioramas and having a Diorama Walk, where all students walk around to view each other's scenes.

6. **Board game**: This creative summative assessment could really be used easily for any subject. Whether reviewing vocabulary, a specific time in history, or standards in math, having students create a board game is a great way to check for understanding. To start, students will decide on the game mechanics. How will it be played and with how many people? Next, students create a game board and any necessary pieces. Then, they create question cards and challenges that showcase their understanding of the topic. They should include an answer key as necessary. Last, students will create clear instructions and a title for their game. You could schedule a game day in your classroom for students to play their games with their peers as a culminating event.

7. **Cereal box report**: Most kids love cereal! Using an empty cereal box, students will cover it with construction paper. The idea is to then invent their own cereal that revolves around the topic being showcased. So, students will come up with a creative title that reflects the key idea of the topic being showcased on the cereal box. Then they will design an eye-catching front cover with the cereal name and an image to go along with it. On the side panels there can be an about section, quiz, or information and facts. The back of the cereal box can be a little more creative with a fun little game or comic strip, or more illustrations. This is a fun way to showcase learning.

8. **Social media fakes**: This would not actually be done on a social media platform but with a paper template or a digital template. Also, using a person would make the most sense, so whether it is

for a character in a story or a historical figure, this type of summative assessment would work best with reviewing a pretend or real-life person. It could also work with concept ideas like the Wanted Posters, but people make more sense. Students pick a social media platform and create a profile name and handle. Then students will illustrate the profile picture and write a description of the person for their bio. Students can include hashtags as well as pretend comments from other characters/people that relate to the profile. You can take it a step further and have them create a series of posts, and even a video post if desired.

9. **Museum exhibit**: A museum exhibit in the classroom is an engaging way to use summative assessment as you allow students to showcase their knowledge through creative displays. After the teaching unit is complete, have students create an exhibit related to what they learned. The exhibit could include a poster, model, diorama, presentation, or even QR codes leading to specific videos explaining the topic. Have each student set up a space for their exhibit in the classroom. When the setup is complete, allow other classes and students to walk through your classroom exhibit! Students will explain their exhibits to the visitors. This type of assessment allows students to show what they learned creatively, as well as explain the process.

10. **Poster project**: No matter the subject or lesson, having students create a poster showcasing their learning can be an excellent way to measure their knowledge of the topic. As the teacher, provide clear criteria for the project, like how much text should be included, how many images should be provided, how many graphs (if any) should be on the poster, and how the poster should be organized. Posters can be presented individually to the class by the students and even hung in the classroom or hallway on a bulletin board.

11. **Video tutorial**: In today's digital age, students are constantly immersed in video content, whether it's on YouTube, Netflix, or social media platforms. By tapping into this familiar and engaging format, having students create their own video tutorials allows them to connect with the standards they are learning in a more personal and relatable way. This type of assessment project allows students to reinforce their knowledge of the subject and apply their

own communication skills as they teach it in a video. Using either a phone, laptop, iPad, or other recording device, students can record their video after they write a script and plan out their report.

12. **Digital portfolio**: A digital portfolio is a collection of student work that is stored and presented in a digital format. Whether using Google Slides, PowerPoint, or Canva, it allows students to showcase their learning. As students are learning about a topic, have them save their projects related to the lessons. Then they can compile them into a presentation. Each piece of evidence that showcases their learning from the topic, whether a quiz, report, creative piece of work, or essay, can be used in the presentation to add to their portfolio.

13. **Newspaper**: Bring actual examples of newspapers, whether digital or print based, to show your class what they will be working on. Explain to students what newspapers are and how they are used to spread information. Students should create a title for their magazine or newspaper. Then they can write several articles that center around the topic being showcased for their learning standards. Students will research their topic and include a news article, opinion piece, interview, and advertisements that are relevant to their topic. These can be as extravagant as you would like, either a single-page report or several pages to create an entire newspaper!

14. **Podcast**: In this type of assessment, students produce an audio-based project where they discuss, analyze, or teach a specific topic. Students can choose the type of format they want their podcast to be. Will they be doing interviews, storytelling, debates, news reports, or even a narrative or document style podcast? Then students can write their script. When finished, they will record their podcast. There are lots of free recording tools, but some of the simplest and easiest include a phone, tablet, or programs like Canva.

15. **Story**: Not only would this type of assessment gauge student understanding of writing and grammar, depending on the topic, it can also measure their understanding of specific standards. Students can write historical fiction, informative stories about a certain topic, or a narrative story that ties in what they have learned. When finished, publishing the stories (which could merely mean printing

them or putting them together in a nice folder) is a fun way to add them to a classroom library for all to read.

16. **Project-based learning (PBL)**: PBL would include students exploring real-world challenges and finding solutions based on what they've learned in class. For example, after wrapping up a unit on geometry, students might be tasked with designing a new playground for school. They will need to measure the spaces available and the size of the play structures being added. While this assesses their knowledge of the math concepts, it can also assess their creative thinking and engineering skills, too.

17. **Game show**: Creating a game show using a computer is a fun way to allow students to not only showcase what they have learned but also teach others, too, as they share it with the class. Whether they create a jeopardy-style game, a quiz show, or some other game show, students will create different categories and write their own questions and answers that support the topic they have learned. Teachers can use the game shows as reviews in class. Students will love seeing their work being used with the class.

18. **Themed choice board**: This is a type of learning tool that provides students with a variety of activities or tasks to complete centered around a particular theme or topic. Usually there are 9–12 choices per board. This is a great way to differentiate as well because you can require different levels of students to complete a different number of tasks. Some students may be required to accomplish three tasks while others may be asked to pick and complete six tasks. The teacher will create a themed choice board that reviews the standard they want to assess. The choice board will offer students a variety of ways to demonstrate mastery of the content at the end of a unit. Whether students choose to design a brochure, write an essay, or create a poster, it is up to them!

19. **Fake website**: Having students design a fake website is an engaging way to have them process their learning and for the teacher to assess their understanding of the topic. Teachers will choose a topic for the website. Then, using a program like Google Slides, PowerPoint, or Canva, students create different slides that represent different pages of their websites. They can even include hyperlinks to link all the

pages together. The website should include pages that explain the topic taught and teach others what was learned. Students should demonstrate a mastery of content learned, while presenting it in a fun and interesting way.

20. **Animated explainer video**: While similar to a video tutorial, the main difference here is that students do not show their face. They may do stop motion or animate characters in Canva. Whatever the case, they are creating an animated story to explain the content they learned.

Incorporating both formative and summative assessments into classroom instruction is essential for meaningful learning experiences. Formative assessments guide the teacher in knowing what and how to teach while summative assessments prove what the students have learned. Both need to work hand in hand to form an effective learning experience. By using ongoing formative assessments, teachers can offer timely feedback, encouraging students to reflect on their learning and take ownership of their growth. Summative assessments help teachers and students know how far they've come and what goals they have reached.

To make assessments truly engaging and impactful, it's important to explore creative approaches that go beyond traditional tests and quizzes. Whether through PBL, digital portfolios, student-designed games, or interactive presentations, assessment can become an opportunity for students to showcase their knowledge in ways that are personal and exciting, rather than frustrating and scary. These creative methods make learning more relevant, allowing students to apply what they've learned in real-world contexts. Ultimately, by combining thoughtful formative and summative assessments with engaging and creative formats, teachers can transform assessment into a tool that not only measures progress but also deepens understanding and sparks joy in learning.

CHAPTER 8

Let's Play: Game-Based Learning

It was my first day as a substitute teacher. It had been a few years since I had taught in the classroom. Since my son was born, we had had two additional children, both girls. I was busy raising my kids at home. Before I knew it, my youngest was in kindergarten, and I was home alone all day. It was a strange feeling. The itch to be in the classroom persisted, and I decided to apply as a substitute teacher in my children's district.

With all my ducks in a row, I got my first substitute gig: a fifth-grade classroom. I was excited because I love the older elementary ages, and the school was near my house, so I wouldn't need to travel far.

When I walked into the classroom, I was a little disappointed because the majority of the substitute lesson plans included Chromebook lessons. So, I wasn't really teaching, but students were on their screens either watching a short video, answering questions, or typing a report. This is *not* what I expected. I was thankful the lesson plans were easy to follow, but I was bored out of my mind, and I could tell the students were not engaged for long either. We made it to the end of the day, and I think we were all relieved to go home.

While I love technology (cue Kip from *Napoleon Dynamite*) and I have even earned my technology education endorsement, there is a time and place for it, and it is not for every lesson. While it might make for easy sub plans, technology for an entire day can be draining. Also, without the proper controls, monitoring an entire classroom on computers all day can be a challenge as well.

I want to emphasize that putting a Chromebook in front of a student is *not* game-based learning (GBL). While it can be fun to use technology, fun does not always equal GBL. Teachers need to be trained how to appropriately use technology in their classrooms. While GBL can use technology (and sometimes it should), it doesn't have to. Also, technology is a powerful tool. I believe students should use it at some capacity every single day. Technology is the world we live in, and it's not going away. Like every tool we hand children, we need to teach them how to use it. Implementing technology into our lessons as a resource aid and not as the actual teacher is the key to appropriate technology use.

GAME-BASED LEARNING EXPLAINED

Simply put, GBL involves using games for the purpose of teaching a specific skill or concept. The game is the central tool for learning the standard, and it can use technology or not. With GBL, students learn through play. I have noticed that when a game is used, students will often be more inclined to participate and may not even realize they are learning at all.

Where and how students use GBL doesn't really matter. They could use online games, interact with physical objects in the classroom, or work as part of a team to reach a specific goal.

When speaking and learning about GBL, it is inevitable you will also hear about gamification in the classroom. While GBL and gamification seem like they are the same, there is one key difference between the two teaching methods. With GBL, the game is the tool to teach the subject. You are learning through play. With gamification, you are enhancing a nongame activity with game-like elements. For instance, a simple GBL activity for kindergartners may be hiding letters throughout the classroom. Students must find each letter and then say the sound to a partner when they find the letter. A gamification example might be as students learn each letter and its corresponding sound, they earn a point. Once they have earned a certain amount of points, they earn a prize or reward. In the GBL example, the kindergarten students are learning through play. In the gamification example, game-like elements (earning points) are applied to a skill or standard the students are learning. See Figure 8.1.

GAME-BASED LEARNING	GAMIFICATION
Teaches a standard through games, not rewards.	Rewards, like points and badges, are earned for reaching goals.
Learning comes from playing the game.	Applying game-like elements to an existing learning experience.
Promotes critical thinking and problem-solving skills.	Points earned can be used for grades and assessment.
Engages learners by making the learning process fun and interactive. Students learn through play and the lessons are immersive.	Engages learners by making the completion of learning rewarding. The motivation to learn is through external rewards rather than intrinsic enjoyment of the activity.

FIGURE 8.1 Game-based learning vs. gamification

SIMPLE GAME-BASED LEARNING EXAMPLES FOR ELEMENTARY STUDENTS

■ **Kindergarten**

Shape Quest: Set up a scavenger hunt where students must find real objects in the classroom that represent different shapes. You can incorporate more skills by asking students to count each specific shape as well.

Garden Math: Set up a small garden area in your classroom where students can "plant" flowers. Use simple equations like 2+3 and let students plant the flowers to represent the equations.

- **First grade**

Word Building Relay: Divide your class into two teams. Position the teams in lines on one end of the classroom. Lay letter cards or tiles on the other end of the classroom, opposite the teams. Call out a word or show a picture, and have the teams race to the letter cards to spell the word. The first team to spell the word correctly gets a point.

Sorting Safari: Students will learn about different animals and habitats. They will then create illustrations of animals in those habitats. Set up different habitat sections in your classroom, which can be as simple as labeling areas "ocean" or "desert." Students will then sort their illustrations into the correct habitat.

- **Second grade**

Math Fact Puzzles: Create puzzles of addition and subtraction facts. Put the math fact on one piece of the puzzle and the sum or difference on the other piece. Students will put the puzzles together either individually or with a partner. You can add an extra gaming element and time students to see how fast they can correctly put their puzzles together.

Rainbow Words: Students are given a die. Each number on the die represents a different color in the rainbow. The color they roll will determine what color they write their word in. This can be used for spelling words, vocabulary words, practicing specific word lists, etc.

- **Third Grade**

Literacy Game Show: Create a digital *Jeopardy*-style game using PowerPoint or Google Slides to review different literacy skills. Use fun themes like aliens, pirates, or safari animals to make it more engaging.

Multiplication Facts Store: Set up a "store" of small items in your classroom, such as cars that are $3, dinosaurs that are $4, small animals that are $2. Then, students can purchase these items and write down their multiplication sentences. For example, two cars at $3 each would be $2 \times 3 = 6$.

- **Fourth grade**

Math Codebreakers: Assign each digit, 0–9, a different symbol. Then write out multiplication facts, division facts, or other math problems, using the symbols. Have students break the codes and solve each problem.

Grammar Charades: Have students play this game in small groups. They are to write different nouns and verbs on slips of paper. Each player takes a turn choosing a slip of paper and acting out that noun or verb. The other students in the group try to guess what is being acted out. Then, the students must determine if it was a noun or verb.

- **Fifth grade**

Math Trashket Ball: Split your class into two teams. Show a math problem on the board and allow teams to answer it. If answered correctly, one team member is given the opportunity to throw a small ball into the trash can. If the ball makes it into the trash can, that team gets one point. The team with the most points at the end wins.

United States Memory Match: Help your students learn the different states and capitals of the United States. Create a set of cards with the names of states and another set of cards with state capitals. Students will shuffle the cards and lay them face down. Then, playing individually or with a partner, they can turn two cards over at a time looking for matches.

GBL includes a vast selection of activities, from simple puzzles and board games to extravagant digital simulations or role-playing adventures. In a future chapter, we will dive deep into some escape rooms and how to enhance the role-playing aspect of GBL. However, understand that with GBL, regardless of the complexity or resources needed, the underlying objective is the same: boost student engagement. GBL is not meant to just make learning more fun; instead, it's about helping students learn concepts by naturally enhancing their problem-solving and critical thinking abilities. With GBL, students are not just passive learners but are active participants in their education.

BENEFITS OF GAME-BASED LEARNING IN THE CLASSROOM

Now that we have a basic understanding of what GBL is, let's talk about its benefits. While substituting in a first-grade classroom, I saw GBL used in a simple yet effective manner. Not only had the teacher nailed classroom management (an important component in any classroom), she had learned how to get students learning together while also encouraging collaboration.

In all classrooms, you are going to find a wide range of learners. Students are going to be on many different levels and achieving different progress. As you are well aware, the teacher is expected to meet the needs of all these learners. One way to do that is to utilize small groups. So, while I was substituting, I was teaching reading groups. I will be honest, I was a little nervous. First of all, my expertise is upper elementary. Second, trusting a sub to lead reading groups means the teacher has confidence her students know routines inside and out. However, no matter the age, students know a sub does not know all the class rules, and there is a chance (a very high one at that) for students to take advantage of their teacher's absence.

However, I pressed forward with the instructions left. Since the teacher had set up such clear routines with her students, and they had obviously been practiced consistently, I really did not have anything to worry about. My lesson plan for the small group was simple: read with the students. The GBL came into play during the other rotations. The teacher had several baskets at the front of the classroom. Each basket was labeled with a name and activity with instructions. Inside each basket were the components of the game. Whether it was a set of cards for consonant-vowel-consonant word and picture matching, a game board to play letter sound recognition, or ice cream word building, students chose a game to play with a partner. There was a paper inside each basket for students to write their work on as well. I loved that the students were able to choose which game they wanted to play.

Why did I like this setup? First, it gave the students the opportunity to review skills. Second, they were able to work with a partner or individually to complete the task. Third, this gave them responsibility and choice since the students got to pick which game to play. I thought this was a brilliant way to incorporate GBL into the school day. I imagine the games are switched out occasionally, with either new games, or to match the season, but are somewhat similar to keep consistency since it was a first-grade classroom.

This brings us to the first benefit of GBL (and my personal favorite): encouraging collaboration. Using game principles in learning can engage students in ways traditional teaching often doesn't. Games are highly motivating and show that learning is about building skills, not just earning grades. Team-based games also help develop collaboration. Since most students enjoy playing games, bringing them into the classroom connects fun with learning.

In a world that is increasingly moving toward online interaction, it becomes even more important for students to learn collaboration with their peers within the walls of a classroom. Learning to work with others is a key skill students need to learn to move forward in this world. It teaches them to collaborate with people, solve problems, and have sympathy for others. What better way to do this than through games?

An example of collaboration within a GBL lesson would be students working together to solve a common problem. For instance, imagine your students are given a quest for an escape room. It reads:

"You are trapped on a deserted island. The map you need to escape is hidden in the metal treasure box before you. To open it, you must solve this puzzle and crack the code."

Puzzles of this nature (see Figure 8.2) encourage teamwork as they appeal to diverse abilities. In any group, there may be a student who excels at math, while another might have a knack for solving logic puzzles. Such games not only reveal natural leaders but also highlight those who can support their peers who face challenges. These varied skills are crucial for learning effective group collaboration.

Another benefit for GBL is the opportunity to offer a safe environment for failure. My own personal experience as both a student and a teacher has taught me that I am scared to fail, especially in front of others. While failing truly is one of the best learning experiences we can have as students and humans in general, it often brings anxiety and stress.

One of the "scariest failing" moments I have had as a teacher happened while student teaching. In retrospect, looking back on this experience, it actually changed my life for the better, but at the time I was mortified.

It was the beginning of my teaching journey. I was in my final year at college and student-teaching a second grade classroom. My entire life

The code to open the treasure box is:

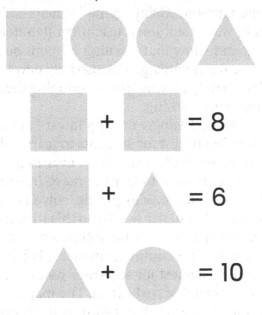

FIGURE 8.2   Treasure box example

I had known I wanted to be a teacher. There was no other career path for me. When I make up my mind, I am determined to reach my goal and will do whatever is necessary to reach it.

When I was assigned to student teach in a second-grade classroom, I was thrilled. I couldn't wait to get started. I had also set up a plan, once student teaching was completed, to get my kindergarten endorsement. Teaching kindergarten was my ultimate goal at the time.

A few weeks in, and I started second-guessing myself and wondering if teaching was really for me. I was terrified to admit this feeling to anyone, so I pressed on. However, I had a very kind and patient professor who eventually approached me and asked if I was enjoying my assignment.

I eventually confessed to her that I was not enjoying this experience and was having a mini crisis because my whole life was always the plan, and now, I didn't know if I liked the outcome. This professor, in her experience and wisdom, suggested I try a different grade. She saw my potential as an educator and didn't want me giving up just yet.

The next day, after talking with my professor, I began student-teaching in a fifth-grade classroom, and my whole perspective changed. First, I knew, once again, what I had always known: I was meant to be a teacher. It just so happened that the older elementary grades fit my personality and teaching style better. Second, after spending a couple months with the fifth graders, my confidence in teaching returned, and I felt reassured that the choices I was making in my career were the right ones. Finally, I learned that it was okay to fail. Without failing, I would never have discovered my passion not just for education but for teaching upper elementary students. Needless to say, I never did get my kindergarten endorsement but fully enjoyed my path as an upper elementary teacher.

Years later, I did eventually have the opportunity to substitute in kindergarten classrooms. I thought maybe being 15 years older and wiser would give me a new perspective. The truth is, it just reinforced to me that my decisions, all those years ago as a student-teacher, were the correct ones. I had to fail to find my success as a teacher, but in the end it was worth it. I did not like admitting to my professor and the teachers I was working with that I was struggling, but it was that experience that led me to be the confident and professional teacher I became.

Failing is a necessary part of growth. It is our failures that lead us to our biggest achievements. However, learning to fail is a necessary skill that still needs to be taught. Using GBL is an excellent way to teach this concept to students in a safe environment.

For example, your students may be playing a game show-style game on the computer that is self-checking. This means, if they get the answer right, they proceed to the next question. However, if they get the answer incorrect, they are prompted to try again. This type of activity, while simple, lessens the stress of failure because students know they can try again if they fail. Like my student-teaching experience, fresh into student teaching and experiencing only one grade as a teacher shouldn't be the determining factor deciding if I am capable to teach. Getting one answer wrong in a game shouldn't determine if a student can really learn or understand a concept. Sometimes, we need to teach multiple grades or answer a question a couple times until we find our success. Perfectionism should never be the goal. Instead, growth through our experiences should be our objective.

Offering the opportunity to fix our mistakes and grow from our challenges is one of the biggest lessons we can learn in school. GBL is the perfect setting to practice failing safely without being embarrassed or put on the spot in front of a crowd. GBL makes failing low-stress and okay. It makes failing part of the learning experience instead of the only outcome.

The next benefit for GBL I would like to touch on is the opportunity GBL gives when encouraging critical thinking skills. Just like it is important to exercise our bodies, it is just as important to exercise our minds. GBL can offer this opportunity to students. When faced with a challenge, students will need to problem-solve to find a solution. Sometimes, this requires trial and error, and other times, it requires students to look at the problem in a new way.

Critical thinking skills and learning to problem solve is an essential skill in the world we live in today. Games are a great way to offer practicing these skills. GBL engages players in scenarios that require more than the basic recall or rote memorization. With GBL students are challenged to analyze and strategize through their work. Whether in the form of a digital computer game, board game, or interactive setup, GBL challenges students to respond to dynamic situations and manage the resources they are given to reach solutions.

Games can also offer a healthy dose of competition. This component encourages many students to work harder, so they either can be the first to solve the problem or even just have the satisfaction of figuring out the puzzle or situation. Games don't have to just be a tool for entertainment. They can be effective resources that provide practical and enjoyable ways to practice critical thinking skills, while reviewing key standards in the classroom.

The last benefit I want to mention in regard to teaching with game-based lessons is that it helps with student engagement and motivation. Rote memorization, for example, with math facts, can be important. A student needs to know their math facts quickly and accurately. It will help when learning harder, more complex math concepts. However, even making these mundane tasks of memorization more fun and engaging can encourage a student to continue learning.

For instance, consider a simple board game that students can play with a partner (see Figure 8.3).

As students roll a die, they will move along the board. The first to correctly reach the summit and answer their facts correctly along the way wins. While students are practicing facts, they are also initiating friendly competition. Students are more engaged while working with the game board and a partner as opposed to going through flash cards or completing a worksheet.

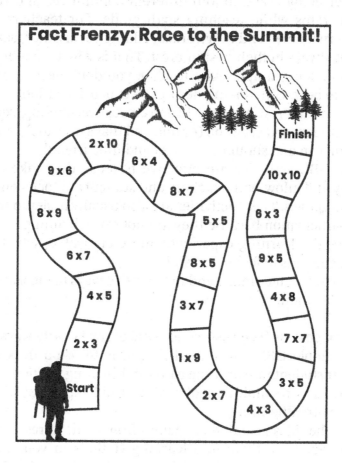

FIGURE 8.3 Fact Frenzy example

GBL provides opportunities for teachers to add fun into their lessons while still keeping the activities educational. Students are actively solving problems that enhance the learning experience and retention of material. Whether it is an escape room, a board game, or a game on the computer, GBL is a great way to get your students engaged and learning.

SIMPLICITY OVER COMPLEXITY: EMBRACING THE UNCOMPLICATED APPROACH

I remember being asked to join different committees and run after-school programs while teaching sixth grade. For teachers who are already overwhelmed and overworked, adding yet another task to their plate is not always in their best interest. That is why I am a huge advocate for GBL being simple! As a teacher, you don't need another task or burden to bear. GBL doesn't need to be expensive or look like it was plucked from Pinterest. You may like to create over-the-top experiences with your students on occasion (or not, and that's fine, too), but making learning fun can and should be budget and time friendly.

Simple GBL activities are effective because they take away the complexity and allow both teachers and students to focus on the core learning objectives. These activities are also usually easier to set up and increase participation because they are not overwhelming to students. This makes the learning experience more enjoyable, which in turn allows the students to feel successful.

Let's go over some simple and inexpensive ways to incorporate GBL into your classroom:

- **Use low-cost or free resources**: One of my favorite ways to incorporate simple GBL into a math lesson is to use a deck of cards. Whether students are drawing cards and creating fractions or setting up math facts, a simple deck of cards can add a splash of GBL to your lessons with little effort.

  Another idea is to find old games from thrift stores or buy them on sale and turn them into learning stations in your classroom. While substituting in a Spanish immersion classroom, I watched students practice their language with each other while playing the game Guess Who. The students would speak Spanish while playing the game and had a list of vocabulary words they needed to incorporate into their questions for their partners. It was an easy and fun way to practice their vocabulary!

- **Digital game templates**: Many websites offer cheap or free game show templates. These templates often have a fun theme like sports or superheroes. Or, they resemble famous game shows from television but revised for the classroom. These games are a great way to insert your own content questions and review standards in any subject with your students.
- **Create your own games to go along with your lesson content**: If you enjoy creating fun and engaging activities for your students, this is a great way to save money. I like to use resources like PowerPoint and Canva to create printable escape rooms or digital game shows as well as Google Forms and Google Slides to create digital escape rooms for students.
- **Student-designed games**: Have you ever considered having students create their own games either digitally or in print ? This is an excellent way to get your students involved in the learning and teaching process. They can create games on their own or with a partner or group. However, teachers assign the topic and students create the game. Then, students or groups can trade games to review standards.

Change can be hard. However, I can guarantee, if you level up your lesson plans a bit and add some fun with games, your students will be thanking you. Not only will you see an increase in engagement, but you will also see students who are excited to come to school, students who are willing to learn, and students who aren't afraid to fail because they know they will eventually find success. Let's get gaming together!

CHAPTER 9

Unlock Digital Power-Ups: Creative Use of Technology in Lesson Planning

Game design for students has come a long way! Many years ago, in the late '90s, my school updated its computer lab. For years, we had those beige-colored computers with black and green screens. The only game on them was Oregon Trail, and we would go to the lab once a week and die of dysentery, cold weather, or snake bites among other things. At one point, a couple of colored MAC computers were added to the lab. If you were one of the lucky students, you got to use a computer with full color. However, the trade-off was you couldn't play Oregon Trail. So, you really had to think about whether getting the full-color computer was worth losing the opportunity to pretend you were a pioneer leading your wagon across the plains with the inevitable misfortune of losing your oxen along the way. I am here to tell you, it was a gamble we all played every single day we went to "Computers class."

Then, in fourth grade, something magical happened: We got a brand new computer lab at the school. I remember our teacher's excitement as she described how lucky we were to have a new lab with computers that all had colorful screens and new programs to help us learn. This was huge! Since there was only one lab, we were allowed to go there once a week. I don't remember a lot about what those computers offered, but I do remember playing one math game on them and doing a lot of typing of reports.

Fast-forward a few years, and I am in eighth grade. My dad comes home and announces we are getting the Internet. "What the heck is the Internet?" I thought. I quickly learned it meant you couldn't use the landline phone but were able to dial up to the World Wide Web. While the intent of getting the Internet was to help us kids with research projects and school, we used it a lot to chat with friends and create email accounts. Thinking back, I have honestly seen a huge progression of technology in my lifetime so far and cannot even fathom what it will become in even a short few years from now.

When I began teaching, the building had one dedicated computer lab. We took our students there on a weekly basis for different computer activities such as typing, learning how to create PowerPoint presentations, and taking online tests. The Oregon Trail was a thing of the past by this point. A few years into my teaching journey, I received my technology in education endorsement. My district had a program called eMINTS, which stood for "Enhancing Missouri's Instructional Networked Teaching Strategies." The program is now implemented across the United States, including in Utah where I was (and am) located. The goal of the eMINTS program is to provide an opportunity to build community in your classroom using high-quality lesson design that is powered by innovative technology.

By completing this program, my classroom would be provided with computers in a 2:1 ratio. I would have one computer for every two students! This was very exciting. With my training, I was to implement technology into my daily lessons and include the use of computers on a regular basis.

Now, even this feels obsolete! In my own children's schools and the district that I substitute teach, each classroom has a set of Chromebooks, so computer labs are now even an outdated relic of times gone by. I am grateful I had two years of training on how to incorporate technology into my teaching lesson plans because, without that training, I believe it would have been easy to fall into what I want to call "Oregon Trail habits," where teachers use computers for fun activities, or as busywork, but don't use the technology to its full potential. I cannot express how hard it is for me to walk into a classroom with technology like smart boards, Chromebooks, projectors, or document cameras and watch a teacher never use any of the technology, unless to have students type a report or occasionally play a random online game. Training on these materials is needed so they can be used to their fullest potential.

When using technology, it is important to make sure the learning outcome is meaningful. There are pros and cons to using both printable and digital game-based learning (GBL) activities. Each type of these activities has a place in the classroom. The key is to tie it into a learning standard, and as an educator you are a pro at this already! So, let's get you confident in using more technology into your lesson plans.

DIGITAL OR PAPER-BASED GAMES IN THE CLASSROOM?

Figure 9.1 lists the pros and cons of both digital and paper-based games in the classroom.

As stated, there is a time and place for both digital and paper-based lessons in the classroom. In an ever-evolving and increasingly tech-savvy world, digital games should be used on a regular basis. However, the key is to make sure standards are being taught and reinforced when playing the game.

A simple game show-style game similar to *Jeopardy* could be used to review math standards. Not only is this engaging, as students earn points for correct answers, but it is also simple for the teacher to assess understanding. As students answer questions, they can write their answers on white boards and hold them up before the class moves on to the next question. I personally love playing game shows with students, because, one, they are easy to implement. Two, students are engaged. Add "game" to any activity, and students are instantly more intrigued. Third, if you can add some friendly team competition, it will motivate many students to try harder.

However, paper-based games definitely have their place! While digital games can be easy, interactive, and full of learning, I love that paper-based games offer collaboration and teamwork. They don't need to be intense or hard to prepare to be effective.

Digital Games

PROS	CONS
• Engaging	• It can take a large investment to get access to the required software or machines
• Accessible for students with different abilities, and can offer them assistive technology when needed	• Technical issues and glitches can occur
• Instant feedback	• Excessive screen time in an already over stimulated era
• Makes data tracking easier and quicker	
• Easy to implement	
• Helps students learn how to use technology in a very tech savvy world	

FIGURE 9.1   Digital vs. paper-based games

For example, here are five simple ideas to add GBL into any lesson plan:

1. **Bingo**: Customize bingo cards for any standard or topic. Use vocabulary words, math problems, spelling words, or historical facts. Use the game as a review or introduction to a new topic.
2. **Question race**: Divide your class into teams. Give each team a different color maker. Tape questions around the room in different locations. Announce the question and allow students to solve the question together with their teams. They will then race to the

Paper-Based Games

PROS	CONS
• Easier to manage as a whole group	• Limited feedback or feedback that is delayed since it requires a teacher to review every answer
• Cost-effective and generally less expensive than digital games	• Requires more storage
• Promotes social interaction	• Time intensive if the game requires a lot of pieces, prep, and set up
• Allows for hands-on learning of standards	• Hard to adapt and often requires an entirely new design of the game for different learners
• Immune to tech failures	

FIGURE 9.1 (Continued)

correct paper and write their answer. At the end, the team with the most correct answers wins.

3. **Story scramble**: Divide your students into pairs. Give each pair a different story that is cut into paragraphs or sentences, depending on length. Time the students to see which pair of students can put the story back together the fastest.

4. **Mystery folder**: Each student or group is given a folder with a question or clue about the lesson. This could be historical facts, math problems to solve, or riddles. Students solve their questions

and reveal their answers to the class. As a class, students use the answers everyone reveals to decipher what the lesson is about.

5. **Codebreakers**: Assign each letter of the alphabet a code. It could be as simple as $A = 1$, $B = 2$, $C = 3$, etc. or giving each letter a specific shape. Then write out questions with the code. Students must break the code to solve the questions.

Want to make any of these activities digital? Simply convert them in programs like Canva or PowerPoint. In today's educational landscape, technology is more than just a tool; it is an integral part of our days and the future. Teachers should be learning how to embed technology into lessons on a daily basis that differs from just having students play a game on a tablet or laptop. There should be meaning. There should be interactivity, and students should be using the computer to develop creative pieces of work to showcase what they are learning.

In today's classrooms, you don't want your students to be just passive observers but active participants in their learning. Embracing technology in the classroom isn't just about teaching students how to use computers; it's also about transforming how they learn, interact, and think about the world. It is teaching them how to safely use technology to benefit not just themselves but their communities, too.

FIVE CREATIVE IDEAS TO INCORPORATE TECHNOLOGY INTO YOUR LESSONS

Here are five ideas for incorporating technology into your lessons:

1. **Student-created videos**: During a unit of study, have students create videos to explain about the subject, teach about it, or showcase what they have learned. Don't just have students type a report; have them present it as a newscast or online story.

2. **Create e-books**: With programs like Canva, creating e-books has never been easier! Have students choose a template or create one on their own. They can add text, images, and graphs to explain what they are learning in class. Students become the author and feel

pride and ownership in the project they have created. E-books can also easily be shared with other classmates and parents.

3. **Stop-motion animation**: I remember when I was in eighth grade and had the option to earn extra credit in my Spanish class. To do so, I needed to create a video. My friends and I decided to do a stop motion with Barbies speaking Spanish. This was in the early 2000s. We were using a VHS camcorder. Stop motion was much more difficult then! Even still, we had a blast. Nowadays, students can set up little stages, use toys, and use apps right on their phones, tablets, or computers! Have students use their characters to explain a topic, tell or story, or create a news story teaching about the subject being learned.

4. **Digital pen pals**: When I was in fourth grade, my teacher announced we were going to have pen pals. We would write these pen pals letters two times a month, and they would do the same. The students were at a nearby school. At the end of the year, our pen pals walked to our school, and we got to meet them in person! This was such a fun way to practice writing, communication, and friendship skills. It is an experience I have never forgotten. With technology, it would be even easier today to hook up with a classroom from another state or country! Instead of a personal meetup, students could do a Zoom meetup at the end of the year. It could create lasting friendships and, at the least, teach students some great personal skills and strengthen writing and communication abilities.

5. **Interactive timelines**: Whether using Google Slides, PowerPoint, or Canva, students can create interactive timelines in your lessons to highlight what they are learning. Whether organizing historical events, tracking scientific discoveries, or recapping a book, timelines are both a fun and engaging way for students to add technology to their learning.

In the end, both digital and paper-based activities must have the same crucial elements to be effective. Each must do the following:

- **Provide value**: The main purpose of any activity, game or lesson in the classroom should support a learning objective. The game must be tied to the curriculum and used to reinforce or teach specific skills.

- **Have clarity**: The rules and the play of the game should be clear. Teachers need to provide explicit instructions for any and all GBL activities. This could be as simple as "While on your computer, you cannot pass the next level until you have answered 10 questions." Or, it could be as intense as a group escape room, which would require instructions on how to work together in the classroom and turn in each puzzle.
- **Be engaging**: Any good classroom game will capture the interest of the students and keep them wanting to learn and continue. It should not frustrate them or cause stress. Often, a compelling narrative helps increase engagement as well as offering some friendly competition. Whether it is the first to the finish who wins or earning the most points, most students enjoy a challenge when there is a goal to work toward.
- **Be inclusive**: As a teacher, you know every student is different and learns at their own pace and in their own style. An excellent GBL activity will provide options for all learners to feel included and successful in some way.
- **Include feedback and assessment**: This is usually easier with digital games where the feedback can be instantaneous. However, paper-based games allow for feedback as well, either through the teacher correcting the work, discussing with students as they play, or reviewing it when the game is finished.

Don't let technology scare you! It is the way of the world, and students need to know how to use it. Think outside the box and incorporate it in new and innovative ways. What can students do besides just typing on the computer? What software can they learn that might benefit them in the future? Had I even had a class on how to use PowerPoint in high school, it would have sped up my learning, rather than having to learn it on my own as an adult. When using technology with your students, ask yourself how it can benefit them now, but also in the future. How can the use of technology help them grow as a person and become a better part of their community?

CHAPTER 10

Level-Up Learning
with Escape Rooms

Several years ago, I was just coasting through my day trying to figure out what I was going to make for my family for dinner, when suddenly, my aunt called, and very enthusiastically said, "I just learned about the coolest activity for students to do in the classroom. They are called escape rooms!" The only experience I had ever had with escape rooms involved being locked in a pirate-themed room with a few different friends and scurrying about trying to solve clues before we became lost at sea. I thought the experience was fun but never really thought much about it after that.

This aunt of mine teaches fifth grade and is actually one of my inspirations for becoming a teacher myself. We often talk about education and bounce ideas off of each other. After giving it some thought, I started to wonder how I could create an escape room for the classroom that brought the same fun and anticipation I felt in my pirate-themed escape room with my friends to life with a group of students and their teacher, who would be leading the helm.

The next day, I quite dropped everything on my to-do list and planned out how an escape room would work in a classroom. After some trial and error, I came up with my first prototype. Believe it or not, it was pirate themed! Students would be reviewing math standards, while working with other classmates to solve clues, codes, and puzzles.

To say the rest is history is an understatement. These escape rooms became a huge hit with students and teachers across the United States.

Having become the self-proclaimed classroom escape game expert, I want to share with you how to create, use and execute lessons with escape rooms.

THE EDUCATIONAL VALUE OF ESCAPE ROOMS

Escape rooms are not just a fun activity; they hold significant educational value by promoting the skills we have been discussing throughout this book such as critical thinking, collaboration, and engagement in the content being taught. These immersive experiences enhance the learning experience for both the students and the teacher because everyone becomes invested in both the journey and the outcome.

In regard to critical thinking, escape rooms require students to think objectively as they solve puzzles and decode challenges. Additionally, escape rooms encourage trial and error as a positive and valuable learning process. Remember how we discussed this earlier? We often learn the best lessons when we make mistakes. One of the key aspects of an escape room is persistence. If you fail a question, you cannot move on, so you have to try again. Students quickly learn that not every attempt will be a success, and they may need to try different strategies to solve problems. This trial and error process, mixed with critical thinking, mirrors real world problem-solving in a safe way where perseverance leads to discovery.

I emphasize collaboration frequently, because it often is a skill that helps students and teachers grow. We learn from others and take the opportunity to listen to new perspectives. With escape rooms, students are working together to solve their puzzles, which means they are combining their collective knowledge to crack codes and escape the scenarios.

Furthermore, as students collaborate and exchange ideas, they develop essential communication skills. Tackling complex problems can feel overwhelming when faced alone, but in a group setting, students learn to value diverse perspectives and actively listen to one another. Through this collective effort, they often reach solutions that might have been difficult to achieve individually.

Escape rooms are also a great way to differentiate for various learning abilities. For example, if you are teaching multiplication in a fourth grade classroom, some students may still be trying to nail down their multiplication facts while others are working on multiplying single digit numbers by double-digit numbers. You can have groups play the same escape game but tailor the questions to meet the needs of each group of students. Or you can also consider how you group your students. If putting together two different levels of games seems daunting, group your students in mixed levels. Allow some students to teach others in the group as they go through the skills being learned in the game. Sometimes, students modeling for each other is the best form of learning.

One of the educational values of an escape room is how engaging and fun they are while still focusing on the learning objectives being taught. The whole experience revolves around a story that requires students to escape a scenario. Whether students are escaping a group of pirates, a silly band of monsters, or a haunted school, the storytelling and mystery aspect of an escape room helps students to connect with the material on a deeper level. They become immersed in the story and excited to escape in the time limit provided. The anticipation of escaping actually creates a natural incentive for students to participate and engage with the activity. Not only this, but often with escape rooms, different teams are competing against each other to see who can escape first. This friendly competition encourages students to stay focused as they work towards a common goal.

CREATING AN ESCAPE ROOM FOR YOUR CLASSROOM

Now let the fun begin! A successful escape room begins with a theme and storyline. When picking a theme, you can consider tying it into what you are learning. For example, if you are doing a unit on the solar system, your escape room theme could involve escaping aliens or a planet like Mars. Or you could have the theme tie into a season. Maybe it is winter, and your students are escaping a giant snow monster! Once you have a theme, develop a storyline that will guide the escape room.

This could involve a rescue mission, a time-sensitive dilemma, or a set of challenges students must solve to escape.

Escape room theme ideas:

- **Pirate Treasure Hunt**: Students must solve all the challenges and find the pirate treasure before a group of mischievous pirates find the treasure first.
- **Time Travel Mishap**: Your class is stuck in a specific time in history and must solve puzzles to return to their present time.
- **Escape the Haunted Mansion**: This is a great seasonal theme for the fall. Students solve all the mysteries to break the curse of the haunted mansion.
- **Jungle Expedition**: An ancient artifact is hidden deep in the jungle. As students complete their challenges, they get closer and closer to the treasure.
- **Secret Agent Mission**: Students are transformed into secret agents and given a top secret mission. They are trying to stop a villain from destroying the city. They must crack the codes to rescue their community.
- **Escape the Museum**: A heist goes wrong and students are now locked in a museum. They must navigate the security codes to escape.
- **Enchanted Castle**: Trapped in a magical castle, students break different spells to unleash codes that eventually lead them to freedom.
- **The Lost Island**: Students have been shipwrecked on a mysterious island. The different teams solve clues and puzzles to find their way to a hidden ship that will sail them back to safety.
- **Space Rescue**: Your students are transformed into astronauts on a malfunctioning spacecraft. They will need to solve their challenges to get back to safety.
- **Escape from Atlantis**: Students must find a way out of the legendary city of Atlantis as it sinks into the ocean.

A second critical component for a successful escape room is how the content is tied into the standards being taught and reviewed in class. The alignment of standards is what transforms the activity from just an entertaining game into a meaningful learning experience. By including the academic objectives within the puzzles, clues, and challenges, students can actively apply what they've learned in a dynamic way.

Whether you are reinforcing math operations, exploring scientific experiments, or practicing language skills, the puzzles and challenges should be designed to promote mastery of specific skills outlined in your curriculum. This would make the escape room not only fun but also a tool for formative assessment. As students play the game, you can watch and see how much the students grasp the concepts. So, as you design your escape game or choose one already created, make sure the escape room has tied objectives and standards clearly into the play of the activity.

The next step in creating an escape room includes designing the challenges, puzzles, and tasks. Often, I think of an escape room as a giant scavenger hunt mixed with clever and well-thought-out clues. Students are given challenges and should not be able to move onto the next one until they complete the one they have, correctly. Clues can even be hidden around the classroom with puzzles on when and where to find them!

There are several types of puzzles you can include in an escape room, but here are some of the most common that I use:

- **Ciphers and codes**
  - *Code wheel*: A code wheel is also known as a Caesar cipher wheel. There are two circles, with the outer circle being the letters of the alphabet, and the inner circle being either the letters of the alphabet or simple images. To create the code, you align a letter from the outer circle with any letter/image from the inner circle. This creates the cipher, meaning a rule for how each letter is coded. For instance, if the outer letter *A* is aligned with the inner circle *D*, the alphabet shifts from ABC to DEF. The word CAT in Figure 10.1 would be FDW.
  - Morse code: Morse code uses a combination of dots and dashes to create a code. Each letter of the alphabet, as well as the numbers 0–9 and punctuation, have their own unique pairings of dots and dashes.

FIGURE 10.1   Code wheel example

- *Substitution codes*: In their simplest form, these types of puzzles require you to substitute a letter for a number or an image.
- *Polybius square*: A Polybius square is a form of a substitution code, where each letter in the alphabet is replaced by a pair of coordinate numbers. See Figure 10.2.
- Pigpen cipher: This is an advanced substitution code, where each letter is represented by a symbol in a grid. The grids used look similar to tic tac toe boards, and X-shaped grids. Each section of the grids is assigned a letter. Each letter is then represented by the shape or part of the grid. See Figure 10.3.

	1	2	3	4	5	6
1	A	B	C	D	E	F
2	G	H	I	J	K	L
3	M	N	O	P	Q	R
4	S	T	U	V	W	X
5	Y	Z	0	1	2	3
6	4	5	6	7	8	9

FIGURE 10.2   Polybius square example

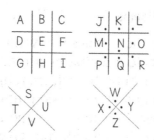

FIGURE 10.3 Pigpen cipher example

- **Riddles**: Riddles are an exciting way to add an extra level of critical thinking to escape rooms. I often incorporate riddles into escape rooms as the clue that tells where the next set of puzzles is located. For example, If I were to hide a set of puzzles near a pencil sharpener, the riddle might be "I give you a point, but I'm not a bee. You get smaller as I work. What am I?" Students love moving about the room and finding new clues based on the riddles they solve.
- **Sequence puzzles**: This is a type of puzzle where students must arrange items or pieces of information into a particular order to solve the challenge. They may involve numbers, letters, words, events, or images. When arranged in the correct order, the puzzle is solved. For instance, students could have a group of scrambled words. They would need to put them in order to create a sentence that explains what their next puzzle is or where their next set of challenges are hidden.
- **Puzzle pieces**: Sometimes, in an escape room, I will even include puzzle pieces. As students put the puzzle together, it will reveal another clue. Or each puzzle piece must be matched to the correct answer to form a finished product.

By using a variety of puzzles and designs, you allow all students and types of learners to succeed. Once you have designed your puzzles, it is time to put it all together! Will you be creating a digital or printable escape room? The setup will depend on which you choose to use. Digital escape rooms often require far less prep, but less collaboration will take place, and students won't move about the room as much.

Digital vs. Printable Escape Rooms

After you have designed the puzzles you want to include, you need to decide if you should create a digital or printable escape room. There are pros and cons to using both. In fact, creating the right environment will help with engagement and immersion into the story. Whether you choose to set up a physical or digital escape room, the setup should align with the standards being taught, your puzzles you've created, and the theme you are tying it all together with.

In a physical escape room, students interact with objects, clues, and puzzles in the classroom space. Students will be in small groups moving together around the room. You may need to move desks or chairs around to encourage movement and teamwork. Some teachers even divide their classroom into zones, and each zone is a different area containing unique clues and puzzles.

Decor is definitely not necessary. However, they can add to the atmosphere and storyline. For example, if you are doing a pirate-themed game, you might consider hanging up some pirate maps and placing clues inside treasure boxes. You could even print a few themed posters to scatter around the classroom.

When using printable games, it's important to gather all the necessary materials and tools in advance. While some escape rooms use lock boxes and key locks, I find it easier to simplify the process by using envelopes or file folders with QR codes. I organize each set of clues into individual envelopes for each group and then strategically place or hide them around the room based on the clues. Students begin with a scenario page that introduces the storyline and leads them to their first set of clues, guiding them through the challenge step-by-step. Students use the information from the scenario page to find their first clue. Once they solve the puzzle in the first set of envelopes or file folders, it will lead them to the next clue, and so on until they reach the final challenge and eventually escape.

The key to a successful escape room is ensuring a smooth and logical progression from one clue to the next. To do this, I like to make sure each clue is clear and leads directly to the next puzzle. Students must solve one puzzle before they can move forward. Often, clues will build on each other too, needing one to solve another. By organizing all the clues in envelopes or folders, it helps the groups stay focused and organized while still maintaining the excitement of an escape room.

Setting up a physical escape room is an activity that doesn't need to be done every day, week, or even month. Instead, they are great activities for the end of units or test prep and review. The method of using envelopes or file folders helps save money on expensive lock boxes but still allows for students to experience an escape room.

As far as escape rooms go, digital escape games offer a more flexible and scalable option with little to no prep. These types of games can be played more frequently and are feasible in any classroom with access to technology. When creating a digital escape, keep in mind they are often created on platforms like Google Forms, Google Slides, or Canva. Students most often do these individually but are still solving riddles, challenges, and puzzles. Just like a physical escape room, students must still think critically and solve a series of interconnected puzzles. These types of escapes are an excellent choice for the classroom because they are easy to set up, can be done anywhere, and don't require physical materials or for objects to be hidden. However, they can still be highly engaging and offer learning experiences.

To begin, you'll need to choose the platform you want your digital escape room to be on. Google Forms is a popular choice because you can add rules to the form that students cannot progress until they enter the correct answer. Since students aren't moving about the room, you can simulate unlocking clues by using Google Forms' Response Validation feature. Or, if you choose to use Google Slides, you can implement hyperlinks between slides and questions.

It is also important to note, whether you are doing a physical or digital escape room, that setting a time limit adds urgency and importance to the game. This type of strategy also adds a bit of friendly competition among students to see how long it takes each group or person to escape. You can project a timer on your board or give students their own timers to see how much time they have left to escape. Whatever you decide, make sure to remind students to check the time occasionally so they can stay on task.

Physical and digital escape rooms both offer unique advantages in the classroom, making them valuable tools for different learning environments. While physical escape rooms offer hands-on activities and encourage movement and exploration, they also foster collaboration and communication among students as they interact face-to-face. On the other hand, digital escape rooms leverage technology and offer a flexibility and accessibility that is hard to achieve with physical games. Digital games are also extremely useful for classrooms with limited resources. Both formats enrich the learning process and promote engagement in the learning material by giving a unique experience through an escape game.

Want to try an escape room with your students? Simply scan this QR code or type the link in your browser to get the bonus material.

teresakwant.com/bonus-material/
Password: levelup

CLASSROOM MANAGEMENT TIPS FOR ESCAPE ROOMS

Escape rooms are exciting and can often bring high energy into the classroom. Just because it is a bit noisy doesn't mean students aren't learning! However, it is important to still keep the class in control. Without proper classroom management, escape rooms can become chaotic or overwhelming. Let's go over some key strategies to keep your escape room running as smoothly as possible:

- **Define roles and responsibilities**: If you decide to have students do the escape room in groups, I suggest giving each team member a role. For example, assign each team a captain, clue tracker, time-keeper, and note-taker. This not only gives students responsibility but helps them stay on task.

- **Before the game begins, explain clear rules and procedures**: Show students how to communicate (what voice levels they should be using), keep the clues organized, move about the room, and, finally, request help from the teacher if needed, and what to do when finished. Also, emphasize that speed is an important component of the game, but the goal is to work together and escape while still being respectful to all team members.

- **Pre-assign groups**: While students might like picking their own groups, if they are pre-assigned by the teacher, you can assure that students are grouped with students of varying levels and that each team has a mix of strengths.

- **Explain expectations for listening and working together**: Show students what it looks and sounds like to listen to their peers and why this is an important aspect of an escape game.

- **Emphasize doing their best work**: Students will want to rush to complete the game. However, keep them doing their best work by requiring them to show all their work on paper, which will also prove they completed each puzzle. Keep the students accountable for accomplishing all their tasks!

While escape rooms naturally are full of energy, it is also important to keep the noise level down so things don't get too chaotic! Right from the start, set a noise rule that encourages students to collaborate without shouting or getting too loud. Also, keep in mind, when students transition between puzzles, make clear instructions how to do so to avoid confusion and students running all over the place.

Another idea might be to implement a "hint station" located at a central place in your classroom. This is where students can ask you questions if they get stuck or need a little extra help. By implementing these strategies, you'll create a smooth and enjoyable escape room for your students. You'll ensure that the activity stays engaging and educational without getting out of control.

The Power of Play in Learning

While doing a winter-themed escape room with fifth-grade students, I remember how excited they were when I introduced the activity we were completing. I started by explaining the scenario: "You have been turned into snowmen, which might sound pretty cool, but there is one major problem: The sun is beating down on you! If you can't solve the math problems in front of you in 60 minutes, you will become a puddle of water. Act fast! You have no time to lose." The students were instantly hooked.

To make sure every group had a chance to succeed, I divided the students into groups of four and carefully mixed ability levels. This way, students with stronger math skills could support those who might need extra help, creating an environment of collaboration and teamwork. No group felt overwhelmed, and every student had an opportunity to contribute. It was incredible to see how this setup encouraged students to not only rely on their problem-solving skills but also lean on their peers when they needed it.

As they opened their clues and started solving the puzzles, the energy in the room was contagious. Students huddled together, talking through the problems and eagerly moving around the room to find their next clue. Every new discovery sparked excitement, and it was clear they were fully immersed in the experience. Watching them work together, strategize, and celebrate small victories as they progressed through the escape room was exciting. The sense of urgency of "melting from the sun," made the learning process feel like an adventure. What started as a fun, winter-themed game turned into a powerful lesson of problem solving, teamwork, and perseverance.

Escape rooms offer a blend of play and education, engaging students in a way that traditional lessons sometimes struggle to achieve. These interactive experiences encourage students to work together, think critically, and apply their knowledge in real-time, problem-solving scenarios. By incorporating puzzles, teamwork, and timed challenges, escape rooms tap into students' natural curiosity and excitement, making learning not only more engaging but also deeply impactful. The benefits of these types of activities extend far beyond the classroom content because escape rooms help build essential life skills such as collaboration, communication, leadership, and time management. They also create a memorable learning experience that students can use to connect with the objectives they are learning.

CHAPTER 11

Tips for Lesson Planning Efficiently and with Purpose

Let's be honest, if I wrote an entire book about lesson planning and didn't include some practical tips and tricks for streamlining the process, I'd be doing you a disservice! Thanks to modern technology, lesson planning has become easier, and dare I say more fun, than it used to be. Whether you're a new teacher or a seasoned pro, lesson planning is simply part of the job description. And while it might not be everyone's favorite task, it doesn't need to consume your life as it did mine during my first few years in the classroom.

I'll never forget sitting in the school library before my first year started, trying to wrap my head around creating a curriculum map for the year. I hadn't even met my students yet and already felt the weight of having to cover all the standards by the end of the year (or really, before testing started). What order should I teach everything? How long should I stay on each topic? Which objectives would be the toughest for my students to grasp? I had all these questions, and more.

With the help of colleagues, we got the year planned out. I remember having a pacing guide with standards I would check off as I taught them. Each week during my prep time on Fridays, I would sit down and look over my curriculum maps. Then I would plan each day and the lessons I needed to teach to stay on track with my pacing guide. While I know I am preaching to the choir, for those who still think teachers just show up and wing it, let me tell you, planning ruled my life those first few years. The amount of work required was intense.

The good news? After about three years, I found my groove. Sticking in the same grade helped because I could start reusing lessons that worked and tweak activities that were a hit with my students. I even came to the point where occasionally I would plan in my head on my way to work, but I probably shouldn't admit that! But, we've all done it! Can you blame elementary teachers though? Between teaching math, reading, writing, grammar, vocabulary, social studies, art, PE, and all the extras to 32 students every day of every week, there's just an enormous amount to accomplish every single day. However, once you find your rhythm, lesson planning becomes less of a chore and more of a creative process. I am here to help you accomplish planning quicker and more efficiently!

To help with your planning, I have come up with an acronym for you to focus on as you create your weekly lesson plans.

P – Prioritize: What needs to be taught for the week?

L – Leverage: Use tools and resources to work smarter, not harder.

A – Adapt: Change happens, and we need to be flexible!

N – Next: Keep thinking ahead of what comes next to reduce last-minute stress.

PRIORITIZE

In a perfect world, you would have a dedicated amount of time each week to plan for the following week. For me as a teacher, it was Friday. Our Fridays were shorter. The students left about two hours early, and the extra time was left for planning. Of course, that time was often filled with not just planning, but copying papers, grading, or talking with teacher besties to let off steam. All necessary (especially the talking with teacher besties part), but that often left little time for actual planning. Short days looked great on paper although they were often overloaded with other tasks. My contract also included some time, about 15–20 minutes each, before and after school where I was to arrive early and stay after the bell for planning. Again, the reality was that was never enough time. So, my planning often spilled into home time. For your sanity, I recommend keeping work at work. The best advice another teacher ever gave me was "When contract time is up, it is time to leave. There will always be something to do. Get your priorities straight, and leave on time."

During the first couple years, this was tough, but once I had my son, I made it my priority to leave school on time. The first step in lesson planning efficiently is prioritizing, and yes, this means prioritizing your work goals and your own mental health and family life as well.

First, with the time you are given to plan, keep that strictly for planning. It can be hard not to get distracted, but if you can plan when you have the time, it won't be overwhelming to teach when the time comes because you prioritized planning! As a teacher, what else should be prioritized in your lesson planning? The obvious answer should be standards and objectives. You will need to look at your curriculum maps and pacing guides and see which standards need to be taught and what needs to be done to stay on task. Often, this means most of your teaching time will be spent in math and language arts objectives with science and social studies sprinkled in. Think about weaving the subjects together. Sure, you are doing a math project, but can it be tied to a science standard, too? Prioritize what can and cannot be taught together.

Another tip for prioritizing your planning is to time-block. Decide on the lessons you need to get planned and organized, and then block out time for each subject to get those lessons planned. In my business life, I like to use a strategy called the Pomodoro technique. The Pomodoro technique helps you improve focus and productivity. The idea is that you break your work into time intervals. I usually do 25-minute blocks, but it could work with 10- or 15-minute blocks, too. You focus on work with no distractions (turn off your phone, don't open your email), and be dedicated to that block of time for planning. Once the first block is over, take a short five-minute break. Maybe you'll go talk to a teacher friend, stand up and stretch, eat a snack, or walk around the school. Then, once your short break is over, you start the next time block. You can do as many cycles as needed until all your planning is complete. So, in your first Pomodoro block, you could plan out all your math lessons for the week. Get the lessons in order and organize the activities you want to use. Then, after your break, during the next session, plan your literacy blocks for the week. This will also help you feel accomplished as you check off items from your to-do list. Staying focused, while taking small breaks, helps you stay refreshed and organized to tackle all your planning!

It is also important to prioritize your goals during your planning period. Your goals will be centered around what your students are learning. Keeping "Must-Do" and "Nice-to-Do" lists can help you focus on what is most important. This can help you from overplanning and focusing on the most essential learning objectives first. If you have a lesson that has a lot of material and activities included, I suggest ranking each part of the lesson from most crucial to least crucial. Then, focus on what is most important first.

You can also use data from assessments, quizzes, and classroom observations to help guide you in planning, too. Focus on what students need support with the most. If you have a regular routine using exit tickets during math, for example, you will have a clear direction on where your students are and in which way your planning should go. Ultimately, using data to inform your priorities in lesson planning will help you more effectively not only plan but also teach for your students. You will be focusing on closing learning gaps and reinforcing key concepts.

LEVERAGE

This is my favorite part of lesson planning: leveraging tools, people, and resources to make your planning smarter, not harder. When I say "leverage," I mean taking full advantage of what's available to streamline your process to save time. Artificial intelligence (AI), for example, might seem intimidating at first, but don't be afraid to use it! While it's not perfect, it can significantly speed up your planning and generate useful ideas or structures that you can refine for your classroom. Another invaluable resource is the network of teachers you work with every day. Your colleagues can offer ideas, share materials, and provide support, so don't hesitate to collaborate and share the load. Teachers love helping other teachers.

Talk to your colleagues and coworkers, ask them how they plan, plan together, share ideas, and work as a team. There is absolutely no way I would have survived my first year of teaching without a mentor teacher and other teachers to collaborate with. Not only did they share great lesson ideas and teaching tips, they were a necessary component to me keeping my sanity on a daily basis.

Beyond people and AI, there are a wealth of tools and resources specifically designed to help with staying organized. From digital platforms like Canva or Google Sheets and Google Slides, these resources can save you hours of work. Without further ado, let's dive into some of these tools to help with productivity and explore how they can make your lesson planning process more efficient.

Canva

First up is my favorite: Canva. Canva is a free tool that can be used by educators. It has evolved over the years from just a design tool to a powerful resource for educators all over the world. While on the outside, its main strength may look like its ease of design features, but that is just the beginning!

Canva has a vast collection of worksheets, slides, lessons, and activities sorted by grade level or subject for teachers to use. Again, this is all for free. In addition, you can edit and change any of the templates to fit your classroom needs. No more finding an activity but it doesn't fit your lesson *quite right* or you aren't 100 percent happy with it. With Canva, templates can be tweaked and modified to best fit your classroom needs.

One of the best features on Canva is its Magic AI functions. For example, with the Magic Write feature, you can type prompts such as "Write me a lesson for third graders all about comparing fractions.

Include a hook, direct instruction, guided practice, and assessment. Make it a pizza fractions theme." You will simply click Generate, and a lesson will appear! You can then create your own worksheets and activities to go along with the lesson. Or search Canva's growing library to find options, too.

Do you like to use a digital lesson planner or a printed one? Good news! Canva can help you create both! Whether you want to create a design that looks like a planner, and use it digitally in Canva, or design pages to print, this program can help you do it. Simply design a template or choose one from their library, and start planning. Canva also allows teachers to easily reuse and adapt their materials. Once you have created a design or project, you can duplicate it, edit it, or repurpose it as needed. Usually, it takes only a few clicks to do so!

On top of this, students can also use Canva. You can build into your lesson plans ways for students to use the program. Magic Studio is a fun way for students to learn simple AI generation tools. Or students can create slides and presentations for reports as well as create posters for display. Seriously, the options are endless for both teachers and students, when it comes to Canva.

Self-correcting Resources

I remember the day I found a website that I could use for my class spelling tests. My students would type their spelling words, and it would instantly correct their tests for me! This saved me at least 30 minutes a week. I was excited to have that time back. The site was called Spelling City; however, you can make these types of spelling tests using programs like Google Sheets or Excel. While it might take time to set it up, in the end it saves you loads of time and sanity.

Whenever you can find a program that can grade for you, I suggest using it. Remember, plan smarter, not harder. In fact, Google Forms is another great option for self-grading materials. You can create quizzes, like multiple choice or true/false options, and assign them to your students. Once students submit their answers, the quiz provides instant feedback to you as the teacher. You can quickly see who grasped the concept and who needs extra help.

ChatGPT

When I first came across ChatGPT, I will be honest, I was a little scared. I instantly thought it would replace every job in America and take over the world. Maybe this seems a little dramatic, but it was mind-blowing, and I was both impressed and overwhelmed. However, as I began to use the tool more often, I realized it was just that: a tool. It's not perfect and often feels robotic, but it can be a great place for generating ideas and in helping with planning.

Here are just a few ideas in how ChatGPT can help you with planning:

- **Custom lesson plan creation**: ChatGPT can create customized lesson plan templates tailored to your subject and grade level. It can also align the lesson plan to specific standards and objectives. Want a fun theme for the season or a holiday? Chat can incorporate that as well.

    Try a prompt like "Can you help me create a lesson plan on (topic) for (grade level)? Include learning objectives for (standard here), activities, and assessments."
- **Lesson materials**: You can ask ChatGPT to help with designing worksheets and practice questions on various topics. It will create these questions quickly and can even tailor the difficulty to match your needs. ChatGPT can even outline an entire unit with guiding questions, project goals, rubrics, and assessments.

    Try a prompt like "Help me create a project-based learning unit with four lessons on (topic) for (grade level). Include questions, project steps, objectives and assessments. Differentiate each lesson to accommodate students with different learning levels."
- **Time-saving features**: Use the AI in ChatGPT to generate multiple versions of your worksheets. This can help you quickly differentiate reading passages or math questions for different levels.

I want to reiterate that AI is not always correct. You will need to read through all the information it gives you and adapt as needed. It might sound convincing and correct, but that is the nature of the program. It is not human and needs a human eye to correct as needed. I often find mistakes, especially in math problems, and need to be careful before I use the material it gives me. AI can also be repetitive and "talk in circles." Make sure you get quality content, and change it to best fit your classroom needs. However, it is an undeniable fact that AI can be an amazing time-saving tool with lesson planning when used appropriately. Don't be scared of it. The more you use it, the more familiar it will become, and the easier it will be to understand.

ADAPT

Adapting in the moment is a crucial skill for teachers as classrooms are dynamic environments where things rarely go exactly as planned. Flexibility in lesson planning allows teachers to respond to the immediate needs of their students, ensuring that learning stays on track even when unexpected changes occur. For example, teachers might have a detailed plan for Unit 2, Lesson 4, but during Lesson 3, they realize that many students are struggling with key concepts and aren't ready to move forward. In this scenario, being willing to pivot and spend extra time on reinforcement or reteaching is vital for student success. Instead of rigidly following a lesson plan, teachers can adapt by revisiting challenging material, offering additional practice, or breaking down the concept in different ways.

To help with planning for spontaneous changes, and let's be honest, they pop up all the time, set aside a couple days for review for each unit. This will give you a buffer if you need more, or even less time, to review specific subjects. You will have wiggle room to make adjustments. Ultimately, as the teacher, when planning, you should always put student needs first. Adapt your plans to ensure those needs are met.

NEXT

Looking ahead is a tactic we should all be using in our daily lives, so applying it to lesson planning should be somewhat natural. One effective way to plan ahead is by using templates for your lesson planning. Whether you create templates in Google Docs or Slides, Canva, or another platform, once you have it set up, it becomes a reusable resource that saves you time and keeps your planning organized. Templates allow you to quickly replicate the structure of your lessons, and if they're digital (which I highly recommend), you can easily copy and paste from day to day. For instance, if you incorporate a "problem of the day" in math, you can simply copy and paste the same format into your lesson plan template, adjusting the problem itself. This not only streamlines your planning process but also ensures consistency in your planning. Templates can also be a lifesaver when you have a substitute. Simply fill in your lesson plan template, and print as needed. This can keep the flow of your classroom running as smoothly as possible with a guest teacher taking over.

Using digital lesson plans becomes particularly beneficial when you can duplicate and customize as needed. Many teachers use a set of slides that they modify slightly each day, adding new content while keeping the format and structure the same. By saving these slides, you build a library of materials that you can reuse in future years, making your planning for upcoming years significantly easier. Once you create a template or set of slides, you've essentially done the hard work up front, and you can benefit from it for years to come. Having a routine and a predictable schedule tied to your template makes it even simpler as you can fill in key information without having to rethink the entire structure of your lessons every time.

Another powerful way to get ahead in your planning is batching tasks. Instead of planning one lesson at a time, dedicate blocks of time to focus on a single task or type of content for multiple lessons at once. For example, you could spend an hour creating your reading lessons for the week or create several week's worth of "problem of the day" activities in one sitting. Hint: leverage that AI! Batching not only helps you stay ahead but also keeps you in the same mental flow, allowing you to work more efficiently and not be overloaded with tasks to complete.

By using templates and batching tasks, you can streamline your planning process. You will be able to focus on delivering high-quality content for your students rather than scrambling on throwing an activity together. Being planned and organized is the key to an effective strategy of planning what's next and looking ahead.

While lesson planning is a critical part of your teaching, it doesn't need to be an overwhelming task that takes up all your time. In fact, if you PLAN appropriately and prioritize, leverage, adapt, and look at what's next, your planning can become a way for you to maximize efficiency for better teaching results. The key is to leverage your technology, collaborate with colleagues, and strategically plan to create a manageable workflow that is consistent and supports your students and your own well-being.

It's important to remember that lesson planning is not just about filling in your schedule with activities; it's about creating meaningful, engaging learning experiences for your students. With tools, templates, digital resources, and batching resources, you'll be able to save time while still delivering high-quality lessons. The more you build these habits into your planning routine, the easier it will become, allowing you to focus on the parts of teaching that bring you joy. Find your rhythm and make lesson planning an enjoyable part of the teaching process!

To help with your planning, I have created some curriculum maps for math and language arts for grades one through five. I realize that not every state, district, school, or teacher uses the same standards and big ideas. In fact, it can be quite varied in the order in which topics are taught from state to state. These are meant to be a guide and reference to help with your own planning. Feel free to copy, modify, and use the pacing guides to best meet the needs of your own students (see Figure 11.1).

1st Grade

	Math	Reading	Language	Writing
Week 1	Understand place value in tens and ones with numbers up to 100	**Literature:** Recognize the beginning, middle, and end of a story	Identify commas in sentences	**Narrative:** Introduce narratives as having a beginning, middle and end
Week 2	Counting to 120 starting from any number less than 120	**Literature:** Identify and describe the characters in a story	Identify verbs	**Narrative:** Introduce characters and settings using simple descriptions
Week 3	Read and write numbers to 120	**Literature:** Recognize the setting in a story and its importance	Capitalize the first word in a sentence	**Narrative:** Use words like first, next, and then to show order of events
Week 4	Compare two-digit numbers using <,>, and =	**Literature:** Understand the central message or lesson in a story	Use periods at the end of declarative sentences	**Narrative:** Revise stories and edit as needed, then complete a final draft
Week 5	Understand the meaning of the equal sign, and determine if equations of addition and subtraction are true or false	**Literature:** Understand how rhyme and repetition contribute to a story	Use question marks at the end of interrogative sentences	**Informative:** Introduce informative writing as having an introduction, facts, and a conclusion
Week 6	Fluently add within 10 using different strategies like counting on and making 10	**Fiction:** Make predictions about what will happen in a story	Use exclamation points to show strong feeling	**Informative:** Focus on grouping similar facts together to support a topic
Week 7	Fluently subtract within 10 using different strategies like decomposing numbers	**Literature:** Compare characters within a story or between two stories	Understand and use singular and plural nouns	**Informative:** Write drafts that introduce a topic and provide basic facts or details
Week 8	Understand the relationship between addition and subtraction using fact families	**Literature:** Use illustrations to gain a better understanding of characters and events	Use adjectives to describe nouns	**Informative:** Revise and correct as needed, and complete a final draft

FIGURE 11.1 Pacing guide

1st Grade

	Math	Reading	Language	Writing
Week 9	Find unknown numbers in addition and subtraction equations	**Literature:** Retell stories, including key details, and demonstrate understanding of their central message or lesson	Use personal and possessive pronouns	**Opinion:** Introduce opinion writing as stating an opinion and giving reasons to support the opinion
Week 10	Add and subtract within 20 using strategies like doubles and near doubles	**Informational Text:** Identify the main topic of a text	Use verbs in past tense	**Opinion:** Focus on giving reasons to explain why students have a certain opinion
Week 11	Solve addition word problems using objects, drawings, and equations	**Informational Text:** Find and explain key details in a text	Use future tense verbs	**Opinion:** Write an opinion piece with a clear statement and supporting reasons
Week 12	Solve subtraction word problems using models and equations	**Informational Text:** Identify and use text features, such as headings, bold print, and captions	Use simple conjunctions to connect ideas	**Opinion:** Edit and revise as needed, and complete a final draft
Week 13	Practice adding within 100 using a two-digit and one-digit number	**Informational Text:** Understand the author's purpose	Use commas to separate the day of the week from the month and the year in dates	**Narrative:** Teach students to add more descriptive details into their stories
Week 14	Add within 100 understanding place value and regrouping tens	**Informational Text:** Use context to figure out meaning of new words in a text	Understand and use contractions	**Narrative:** Focus on writing clear beginnings and endings that complete a story
Week 15	Practice subtracting multiples of 10 from multiples of 10, up to 100	**Informational Text:** Compare two texts on the same topic to find similarities and differences	Use articles to specify nouns	**Narrative:** Introduce simple dialogue in stories
Week 16	REVIEW WEEK	**Informational Text:** Explore how illustrations or pictures provide additional information in text	Identify and use simple prepositions	**Narrative:** Revise and edit, then complete a final draft

FIGURE 11.1 (Continued)

1st Grade

	Math	Reading	Language	Writing
Week 17	Measure lengths using non-standard units	**Informational Text:** Understand the sequence of events or steps in a text	Recognize and form compound words	**Informative:** Write about a topic by grouping related information together
Week 18	Compare objects being measured	**Informational Text:** Summarize key details and main ideas	Use apostrophes	**Informative:** Include simple facts and details to explain a topic clearly
Week 19	Order measured objects by length	**Literature:** Identify and describe the major events in a story	Sort words into categories to help understand meaning	**Informative:** Use labels or simple diagrams to enhance explanations
Week 20	Tell and write time in hours using digital and analog clocks	**Literature:** Understand how repetition in poems or stories can emphasize important ideas	Use synonyms to replace commonly used words	**Informative:** Revise and edit as needed, and complete a final draft
Week 21	Tell and write time in half-hours using digital and analog clocks	**Literature:** Identify common patterns in fairy tales	Use antonyms to expand vocabulary	**Opinion:** Expand reasons to provide more detail
Week 22	Identify coins recognizing pennies, nickels, dimes, and quarters	**Literature:** Identify rhyming patterns in poems or stories	Use alphabetical order to arrange words	**Opinion:** Focus on organizing an opinion paragraph
Week 23	REVIEW WEEK	**Literature:** Compare and contrast stories from different cultures, focusing on themes	Identify root words to understand related words	**Opinion:** Write concluding statements that restate an opinion
Week 24	Define attributes of shapes, such as the number of sides and corners	**Literature:** Make inferences about how a character might act based on their actions	Ensure subjects and verbs agree	**Opinion:** Revise and edit as needed, and complete a final draft

FIGURE 11.1   (Continued)

1st Grade

	Math	Reading	Language	Writing
Week 25	Draw 2D shapes like squuares, triangles, rectangles, and circles	**Literature:** Recognize how dialogue reveals character traits	Use pronouns to replace nouns	**Narrative:** Describe character's feelings with actions
Week 26	Build shapes to possess defining attributes	**Literature:** Identify common patterns in fairy tales	Form and use irregular plural nouns	**Narrative:** Focus on sensory details to describe setting and events in more detail
Week 27	Compose new shapes by combining simple 2D shapes	**Literature:** Retell familiar stories focusing on the beginning, middle, and end	Understand subtle difference between similar verbs	**Narrative:** Write clear conclusions to provide closure to a story
Week 28	Explore 3D shapes like cone, cylinders, cubes, and spheres	**Informational:** Identify the most important information in a text	Use common adverbs to describe how actions are performed	**Narrative:** Edit and revise as needed, and complete a final draft
Week 29	Partition shapes into equal parts, focusing on halves and quarters	**Informational:** Identify cause and effect	Use common prefixes to change the meaning of words	**Informative:** Write multiple sentences that explain a topic clearly
Week 30	Recognize that when a shape is partitioned into two or four equal parts, each part is a half or a quarter of a whole	**Informational:** Learn to use diagrams or charts to find information in a text	Use surrounding words and sentences to determine the meaning of an unknown word	**Informative:** Incorporate basic headings into writing
Week 31	REVIEW WEEK	**Informational:** Use context clues to figure out the meaning of unfamiliar words in a text	Practice using alphabetical order with word lists	**Informative:** Write an informative text
Week 32	Collect data by asking and answering questions like "How many?" or "Which is more?"	**Informational:** Understand how ideas and events are connected	add -ed and -ing to base words and understand how theses endings change meaning	**Informative:** Revise and edit as needed, and complete a final draft

FIGURE 11.1 (Continued)

1st Grade

	Math	Reading	Language	Writing
Week 33	Represent data using simple charts and tally marks to organize information	**Informational:** Compare two informational texts on the same topic	Use a glossary or beginning dictionary to find the meaning of unknown words	**Opinion:** Come up with several reasons to support an opinion
Week 34	Use picture graphs and understand how the pictures are used to represent and interpret data	**Informational:** Revisit text features like headings, captions and bold print	Review common long vowel patterns	**Opinion:** Focus on organizing opinions with an introduction, reasons and conclusion
Week 35	Solve problems based on data collected	**Informational:** Understand the author's purpose	Review common short vowel patterns	**Opinion:** Peer edit and revise
Week 36	REVIEW WEEK	**Informational:** Summarize key details and the main topic from a text	Practice writing sentences that flow smoothly	**Opinion:** Complete a final draft

FIGURE 11.1 (Continued)

2nd Grade

	Math	Reading	Language	Writing
Week 1	Understand place value of two-digit numbers	**Literature:** Recognize story elements, such as characters, setting, and plot	Identify and use common nouns and verbs	**Narrative:** Introduce the narrative structure focusing on beginning, middle and end
Week 2	Skip-count within 1,000	**Literature:** Identify and describe characters based on their thoughts, words, and actions	Correctly use capitalization, including proper nouns and the beginnings of sentences	**Narrative:** Introduce describing characters and settings using basic details and sensory words
Week 3	Understand odd and even numbers	**Literature:** Understand the central message or lesson in a story	Understand and write simple sentences	**Narrative:** Write events in order using "first," "next," and "then"
Week 4	Compare two- and three-digit numbers	**Literature:** Understand how repeated phrases contribute to a story	Use commas to separate items in a list	**Narrative:** Revise and edit writing
Week 5	Add and subtract within 20	**Literature:** Learn how illustrations enhance understanding of characters and setting	Form and use plural nouns, including irregular plural nouns	**Informative:** Introduce the informative structure focusing on introductions, facts and conclusions
Week 6	Add and subtract within 100 fluently	**Literature:** Identify the basic structure of a story (beginning, middle, end)	Use regular and irregular past tense verbs	**Informative:** Begin gathering information from text to use in writing
Week 7	Use addition to find the total number of objects in arrays	**Literature:** Compare and contrast two or more versions of the same story	Identify and use adjectives to describe nouns	**Informative:** Write drafts that include a topic sentence and supporting facts or details
Week 8	Add up to four two-digit numbers	**Literature:** Summarize the key elements of a story	Use the correct punctuation for different types of sentences	**Informative:** Revise and edit writing

FIGURE 11.1 (Continued)

2nd Grade

	Math	Reading	Language	Writing
Week 9	REVIEW WEEK	**Literature:** Describe the setting of a story and its importance to the plot	Understand and form compound words	**Opinion:** Introduce the opinion structure focusing on stating an opinion, giving reasons, and providing a conclusion
Week 10	Add within 1,000	**Literature:** Compare and contrast two or more versions of the same story	Use subject and object pronouns correctly in sentences	**Opinion:** Teach students to give reasons that support their opinions
Week 11	Subtract within 1,000	**Informational Text:** Identify the main topic in a text	Identify and use synonyms and antonyms	**Opinion:** Write a complete opinion with supporting reasons
Week 12	Mentally add and subtract 10 or 100	**Informational Text:** Recognize and use text features like captions, headings, and bold words to find information	Use different verb tenses correctly (past, present, future)	**Opinion:** Revise and peer edit
Week 13	Fluently add and subtract within 100	**Informational Text:** Compare and contrast two informational texts on the same topic	Understand and use common abbreviations	**Narrative:** Focus on writing narratives with more detailed events and logical sequencing
Week 14	Solve word problems involving addition and subtraction	**Informational Text:** Use context clues to understand new vocabulary	Identify and use adverbs to describe actions	**Narrative:** Use dialogue and description to expand stories
Week 15	Use addition to find unknown values in equations	**Informational Text:** Understand why an author writes an informational text	Understand and distinguish between common homophones	**Narrative:** Focus on writing clear conclusions to wrap up narratives
Week 16	Use subtraction to find unknown values in equations	**Informational Text:** Describe the connection between events or ideas in a text	Identify and understand common prefixes and suffixes	**Narrative:** Revise, edit, and complete a final draft

FIGURE 11.1　(Continued)

2nd Grade

	Math	Reading	Language	Writing
Week 17	Solve two-step word problems	**Informational Text:** Review text features and how they help find important information	Understand and write compound sentences	**Informative:** Write paragraphs with clear topic sentences and supporting facts
Week 18	Measure lengths using appropriate tools	**Informational Text:** Summarize key facts from a text	Use apostrophes for form contractions correctly	**Informative:** Focus on including facts, definitions, and simple explanations
Week 19	Estimate lengths using units	**Literature:** Learn how a character's actions move a story forward	Interpret words with multiple meanings based on context	**Informative:** Introduce simple text features like headings or pictures to support writing
Week 20	Compare lengths and solve word problems	**Literature:** Analyze how dialogue reveals character traits	Understand how to select words that are appropriate for different contexts	**Informative:** Revise, edit, and complete a final draft
Week 21	Tell and write time to the nearest five minutes	**Literature:** Identify rhyme and rhythm patterns in poems and stories	Identify the meaning of common root words to determine the meaning of new words	**Opinion:** Practice expanding reasons with details and evidence
Week 22	Count money and solve word problems with money	**Literature:** Understand how stories from different cultures share similar themes and lessons	Apply the meaning of a known root word as a strategy to break down and understand more complex words in reading	**Opinion:** Focus on organizing writing with clear reasons and a concluding statement
Week 23	Generate and represent measurement data	**Literature:** Understand how repeated phrases in fables emphasize lessons	Understand and use common suffixes	**Opinion:** Practice writing simple conclusions that restate the opinion
Week 24	REVIEW WEEK	**Literature:** Identify common patterns in fairy tales	Understand and use collective nouns	**Opinion:** Revise, edit, and complete a final draft

FIGURE 11.1 (Continued)

2nd Grade

	Math	Reading	Language	Writing
Week 25	Identify and draw shapes	**Literature:** Summarize a story by focusing on key events	Form and use compound words to enhance writing	**Narrative:** Develop characters using descriptions
Week 26	Explore 2D shapes and how they relate to each other	**Literature:** Predict how characters will react to events based on their traits	Use reflexive pronouns like "myself" and "yourself" in writing	**Narrative:** Use sensory details to expand writing
Week 27	Partition shapes into equal parts	**Literature:** Compare and contrast two versions of the same story	Use context to determine the meaning of unfamiliar words	**Narrative:** Focus on writing clear endings that provide closure
Week 28	Work with fractions as equal parts of a whole	**Informational Text:** Understand the sequence of events in a text	Distinguish between shades of meaning among closely related verbs	**Narrative:** Revise, edit, and complete a final draft
Week 29	Relate fractions to division of shapes	**Informational Text:** Revisit identifying the main idea and supporting details in a text	Create compound sentences using conjunctions like "and," "but," and "or."	**Informative:** Write two or more paragraph essays with clear topic sentences
Week 30	Explore basic concepts of cubes, cones, spheres, and cylinders	**Informational Text:** Use diagrams, charts and other visuals to gather information from a text	Use irregular past tense verbs correctly in sentences	**Informative:** Add simple text features like headings, labels, or captions
Week 31	REVIEW WEEK	**Informational Text:** Identify cause and effect relationships in a text	Use apostrophes to form singular and plural possessive nouns	**Informative:** Organize ideas using facts and details
Week 32	Represent and Interpret data using bar graphs, picture graphs, and tally charts	**Informational Text:** Use context to identify the meaning of new words	Use adjectives to make comparisons	**Informative:** Revise, edit, and complete a final draft

FIGURE 11.1   (Continued)

2nd Grade

	Math	**Reading**	**Language**	**Writing**
Week 33	Solve problems using graphs and interpreting data to answer questions	**Informational Text:** Identify reasons an author gives to support a point	Recognize and spell irregularly spelled words	**Opinion:** Teach students to come up with multiple reasons to support opinions
Week 34	Compare data with picture and bar graphs	**Informational Text:** Compare and contrast the information given in two texts on the same topic	Use a dictionary to find the meanings of unknown words	**Opinion:** Organize opinion writing with clear structure
Week 35	Review generating measurement data and using line plots	**Informational Text:** Revisit key details in texts and how they support the main idea	Use commas and quotation marks correctly in dialogue	**Opinion:** Use conclusions to tie the writing piece together
Week 36	REVIEW WEEK	**Informational Text:** Summarize text using key details and main ideas	Combine short sentences to form longer, more detailed sentences	**Opinion:** Revise, edit, and complete a final draft

FIGURE 11.1   (Continued)

3rd Grade

	Math	**Reading**	**Language**	**Writing**
Week 1	Understanding place value within 1,000 and rounding	**Literature:** Identify the basic structure of a story (beginning, middle, end)	Understanding capitalization rules for sentences and proper nouns	**Narrative:** Introduce narrative elements like characters, setting, and plot
Week 2	Using place value to add multi-digit numbers with regrouping	**Literature:** Analyze how characters, setting and plot interact in a story	Using correct punctuation marks (periods, question marks, exclamation points)	**Narrative:** Use graphic organizers to plan narratives
Week 3	Using place value to subtract multi-digit numbers with regrouping	**Literature:** Determine the central message or lesson of a story, fable, or folktale	Using commas when writing addresses	**Narrative:** Use dialogue to develop events and transitions
Week 4	Understanding multiplication as repeated addition using arrays and equal groups	**Literature:** Identify and describe character traits and how they influence a story	Identify and use regular and irregular plural nouns	**Narrative:** Peer editing and revising. Writing a final narrative draft
Week 5	Learning multiplication facts 0s, 1s, and 2s using models and patterns	**Literature:** Identify the narrator's or character's point of view in a story	Understanding pronouns and their use in sentences	**Informative:** Introduce the structure of informative writing
Week 6	Using division as equal sharing and its relationship to multiplication	**Literature:** Explain how illustrations contribute to the meaning of a story	Identify and use verbs in sentences, including action verbs	**Informative:** Gather information and take notes for an informative writing piece
Week 7	Learning multiplication and division facts for 3s, 4s, and 9s using models and skip counting	**Literature:** Identify and understand literal and nonliteral language in stories	Recognize and use regular and irregular verbs in past tense	**Informative:** Write a draft with a clear topic sentence, supporting details, and conclusion
Week 8	Learning multiplication and division facts for 5s and 10s using skip counting and models	**Literature:** Summarize a story, identifying important characters, setting, and plot details	Understanding past, present, and future verb tenses	**Informative:** Revise and peer edit. Create final draft

FIGURE 11.1   (Continued)

3rd Grade

	Math	Reading	Language	Writing
Week 9	Learning multiplication and division facts for 6s, 7s, and 8s using skip counting and models	**Literature:** Compare and contrast characters in a story and how they react to events	Write compound sentences using conjunctions	**Opinion:** Introduce opinion writing
Week 10	REVIEW WEEK	**Informational Text:** Identify and use text features like headings, captions, and diagrams	Identify and write declarative, interrogative, imperative, and exclamatory sentences	**Opinion:** Introduce opinion writing
Week 11	Understanding and applying the commutative property of multiplication	**Informational Text:** Identify the main idea in an informational text and explain how key ideas support it	Write simple and compound sentences with proper punctuation	**Opinion:** Write a draft of an opinion piece with an introduction, supporting details and conclusion
Week 12	Applying the associative property to solve multiplication problems	**Informational Text:** Identify cause and effect relationships	Write and use adjectives to describe nouns	**Opinion:** Peer edit and create a final draft of an opinion writing piece
Week 13	Using the distributive property to break down more complex multiplication problems	**Informational Text:** Identify the sequence of events or steps in a process	Form and use comparative and superlative adjectives correctly	**Narrative:** Create problems and solutions within a narrative story
Week 14	Solving two-step word problems involving multiplication and division	**Informational Text:** Identify the author's purpose to inform, explain, entertain, or persuade	Identify and use adverbs to describe actions	**Narrative:** Practice writing hooks to draw in readers
Week 15	Understanding fractions as numbers and representing them on number lines	**Informational Text:** Use diagrams, charts, maps, and visuals to help understand the text	Form and use comparative and superlative adverbs correctly	**Narrative:** Focus on writing satisfying conclusions to resolve a narrative
Week 16	Representing and comparing fractions on a number line	**Informational Text:** Determine the meaning of specific vocabulary	Ensure subjects and verbs agree in sentences	**Narrative:** Peer edit and creating final narrative projects

FIGURE 11.1 (Continued)

3rd Grade

	Math	Reading	Language	Writing
Week 17	Comparing fractions with the same numerator and denominator	**Informational Text:** Summarize key points and details	Ensure pronouns agree with their antecedents	**Informative:** Write paragraphs with topic sentences and supporting details
Week 18	Using visual models and reasoning to compare fractions	**Informational Text:** Compare and contrast key points across two text on the same topic	Use quotation marks correctly in dialogue	**Informative:** Work on including facts, definitions, and examples into the writing projects
Week 19	Solving word problems that involve fractions and whole numbers	**Literature:** Make inferences about characters, settings, and events based on text evidence	Form and use possessive nouns	**Informative:** Use transitions to connect ideas
Week 20	REVIEW WEEK	**Literature:** Describe the setting of a story and how it impacts the characters and plot	Form and use contractions correctly	**Informative:** Peer edit and writing final drafts to publish
Week 21	Understanding area as covering space and its relationship to multiplication	**Literature:** Identify cause and effect relationships in a story	Understand how prefixes change the meaning of words	**Opinion:** Develop persuasive techniques. Learn about addressing opposing viewpoints
Week 22	Using multiplication to find the area of rectangles	**Literature:** Use text evidence to support inferences with evidence from the story	Understand how suffixes change the meaning of words	**Opinion:** Provide examples to support opinions
Week 23	Relating area to addition and solving world problems involving area	**Literature:** Identify and analyze how dialogue contributes to character development and plot	Use root words to determine the meaning of new words	**Opinion:** Write conclusions to restate opinions and emphasize reasons
Week 24	Understanding perimeter as the total distance around a polygon	**Literature:** Compare and contrast themes in stories by the same or different authors	Use synonyms to enhance writing and understanding of shades of meaning	**Opinion:** Peer edit for clarity and write final pieces

FIGURE 11.1 (Continued)

3rd Grade

	Math	Reading	Language	Writing
Week 25	Solving real-world problems involving both area and perimeter	**Literature:** Identify and interpret similes and metaphors in stories	Understand and use antonyms to improve vocabulary	**Narrative:** Write narrative with descriptive language and deeper character development
Week 26	Telling time to the nearest minute and calculating elapsed time	**Literature:** Recount key details and events in a story to understand the theme	Recognize and use homophones in context	**Narrative:** Incorporate similes, metaphors, and vivid descriptions into the writing
Week 27	Solving real-world problems involving time intervals	**Literature:** Gather information from a story to form conclusions	Understand and use words with multiple meanings	**Narrative:** Practice building suspense and creating resolutions
Week 28	REVIEW WEEK	**Informational Text:** Explain connections among historical events, scientific ideas, or steps in a process	Explore and understand common idioms	**Narrative:** Peer edit and write final projects
Week 29	Creating and interpreting bar graphs and picture graphs	**Informational Text:** Make inferences based on text evidence	Understand proverbs and their meanings	**Informative:** Write multi-paragraph essays with clear organization
Week 30	Creating and interpreting line plots using measurement data	**Informational Text:** Support answers and conclusions with evidence from the text	Use figurative language like similes and metaphors	**Informative:** Incorporate headings, diagrams, and captions
Week 31	Measuring liquid volumes using standard units (liters and milliliters)	**Informational Text:** Identify cause and effect relationships in informational texts	Review prefixes, suffixes, and root words	**Informative:** Draft an essay with researched facts
Week 32	Measuring the mass of objects using standard units (grams and kilograms)	**Informational Text:** Identify sequence of events	Use context clues to understand new vocabulary	**Informative:** Peer edit and publish final essays

FIGURE 11.1 (Continued)

3rd Grade

	Math	Reading	Language	Writing
Week 33	Solving real-world problems involving mass and volume	**Informational Text:** Compare and contrast key points from two informational texts on the same topic	Explore word relationships through synonyms, antonyms, and homophones	**Opinion:** Research facts to support opinions
Week 34	Understanding and identifying the attributes of different shapes, including quadrilaterals	**Informational Text:** Summarize the main idea and key details from the text	Practice combining and expanding sentences	**Opinion:** Write opinions to stay focused on the main point
Week 35	Partitioning shapes into parts with equal areas and understanding fractional parts of shapes	**Informational Text:** Gather information from multiple sources or sections of nonfiction text to arrive at a conclusion	Review and reinforce grammar and language conventions	**Opinion:** Write final drafts with a clear structure and persuasive points
Week 36	REVIEW WEEK	**Informational Text:** Explain how key details support the main idea of a text	REVIEW WEEK	**Opinion:** Peer edit and create final drafts

FIGURE 11.1 (Continued)

4th Grade

	Math	Reading	Language	Writing
Week 1	Recognize and understand the value of each digit in multi-digit numbers	**Literature:** Recognize story components like characters, setting, and plot	Review nouns, verbs, adjectives, and adverbs	**Narrative:** Introduce narrative elements like characters, setting, and plot
Week 2	Compare and order multi-digit numbers	**Literature:** Identify and understand themes in stories	Understand simple and compound sentences	**Narrative:** Use graphic organizers to plan narratives
Week 3	Round multi-digit numbers to any place value	**Literature:** Compare and contrast two or more characters, settings, or events in a story	Use proper end punctuation	**Narrative:** Use dialogue to describe and develop events, characters and plot
Week 4	Add multi-digit numbers using the standard algorithm	**Literature:** Understand the narrator's point of view and how it affects the story	Use the correct form of capitalization in sentences	**Narrative:** Peer editing and revising, and writing a final narrative draft
Week 5	Subtract multi-digit numbers using the standard algorithm	**Literature:** Explore how poetry differs from prose and how its structure influences meaning	Understand and use subject, object, and possessive pronouns	**Informative:** Introduce the structure of informative writing with an introduction, body with facts, and conclusion
Week 6	Apply addition and subtraction skills to solve real world word problems	**Literature:** Identify and analyze figurative language and how it's used in literature	Use commas to join clauses in compound sentences	**Informative:** Research a topic and gather relevant information, and organize into notes
Week 7	REVIEW WEEK	**Literature:** Summarize key events in a story	Distinguish between adjectives and adverbs and their usage	**Informative:** Write a draft with a clear topic sentence, supporting details, and conclusion
Week 8	Identify factors of whole numbers	**Literature:** Compare and contrast stories in the same genre or that have similar themes or topics	Understand how to use quotation marks in dialogue and for direct quotes	**Informative:** Revise and peer edit, then create final draft

FIGURE 11.1 (Continued)

4th Grade

	Math	Reading	Language	Writing
Week 9	Identify multiples of whole numbers	**Literature:** Compare stories that have contrasting themes	Identify and use prepositional phrases	**Opinion:** Introduce opinion writing with a clear opinion, reasons, and evidence
Week 10	Recognize numbers patterns	**Informational Text:** Identify the main idea in a text and how key details support it	Practice combining simple sentences into compound and complex sentences	**Opinion:** Practice linking opinions with clear reasons and supportive transition words
Week 11	Understand multiplication as repeated addition and solve real world problems	**Informational Text:** Summarize texts, focusing on main ideas and key details	Use and understand synonyms and antonyms in writing	**Opinion:** Write a complete draft of an opinion piece with a clear opinion, supporting reasons, and a conclusion
Week 12	Identify and use patterns in multiplication	**Informational Text:** Understand and describe cause and effect in informational text	Use and understand similes and metaphors in writing	**Opinion:** Peer edit and create a final draft of an opinion writing piece
Week 13	Multiply multi-digit problems using various strategies including the standard algorithm	**Informational Text:** Analyze the use of text features like headings, diagrams, and captions	Correctly form and use comparative and superlative adjectives	**Narrative:** Focus on creating problems, events, and resolutions in a narrative
Week 14	Solve real world problems involving multiplication of multi-digit numbers	**Informational Text:** Use context clues to determine the meaning of unknown words	Identify and use coordinating and subordinating conjunctions	**Narrative:** Craft engaging hooks to draw readers into a story
Week 15	Understand division as repeated subtraction and partitioning	**Informational Text:** Determine the author's point of view in the text	Use context clues to determine the meaning of unknown words	**Narrative:** Write conclusions that resolve a story
Week 16	Practicing long division with multi-digit numbers and no remainders	**Informational Text:** Compare and contrast information from two different texts on the same topic	Determine and understand the meanings of common prefixes and suffixes	**Narrative:** Peer edit and create a final writing draft

FIGURE 11.1 (Continued)

4th Grade

	Math	Reading	Language	Writing
Week 17	Solve long division problems with remainders	**Informational Text:** Understand and describe cause and effect in informational text	Understand and use root words to build vocabulary	**Informative:** Introduce writing multi-paragraph essays with clear organization
Week 18	Solve real world word problems involving division	**Informational Text:** Gather information from multiple sources on the same topic to develop a deeper understanding	Understand and use idioms in context	**Informative:** Include facts, definitions, and examples in the explain ideas
Week 19	Review Week	**Literature:** Examine how a story's plot develops over time, focusing on the sequence of events	Understand and distinguish between homophones in writing	**Informative:** Incorporate headings, diagrams, and captions to clarify information
Week 20	Find equivalent fractions and simplify fractions	**Literature:** Make inferences and draw conclusions using evidence from the text	Expand vocabulary through context and word analysis	**Informative:** Revise and peer edit. Create a final writing draft
Week 21	Compare fractions with like denominators	**Literature:** Describe the setting in a story, focusing on how it affects the plot and characters	Form compound words	**Opinion:** Introduce counterarguments in opinion writing
Week 22	Compare fractions with unlike denominators	**Literature:** Explore the use of symbolism in stories	Practice varying sentence length and structure	**Opinion:** Use examples and evidence to support reasons
Week 23	Add fractions with like and unlike denominators	**Literature:** Identify the use of figurative language in literature	Review similes, metaphors, and idioms	**Opinion:** Write persuasive conclusions to restate and emphasize opinions
Week 24	Subtract fractions with like denominators	**Literature:** Compare and contrast themes in literature, drawing on evidence from multiple sources	Choose words and phrases to convey ideas	**Opinion:** Revise and peer edit. Write a final draft

FIGURE 11.1 (Continued)

4th Grade

	Math	Reading	Language	Writing
Week 25	Add and subtract mixed numbers	**Literature:** Compare different narrative structures	Review and apply knowledge of prefixes, suffixes, and root words	**Narrative:** Focus on developing characters through thoughts, words, and actions
Week 26	Add and subtract mixed numbers. Convert improper fractions and mixed numbers	**Literature:** Explain how words help set the mood or tone in a story and provide imagery	Use figurative language in writing	**Narrative:** Use figurative language to enhance descriptions in writing
Week 27	Multiply fractions by whole numbers	**Literature:** Explore themes by connecting them to characters and plot development	Explore and apply word relationships in writing	**Narrative:** Build suspense in narratives and craft satisfying resolutions
Week 28	Solve real-world problems multiplying fractions by whole numbers	**Informational Text:** Distinguish between facts and opinions in text	Understand and use proverbs and adages in context	**Narrative:** Peer edit and create final writing draft
Week 29	Use decimal notation for fractions with denominators 10 or 100	**Informational Text:** Evaluate an author's argument and reasoning in a text	Reinforce basic parts of speech	**Informative:** Focus on writing multi-paragraph informative essays
Week 30	Compare decimals to the hundredths place	**Informational Text:** Explain the chronological order of events in a text	Practice combining sentences for clarity and flow	**Informative:** Incorporate diagrams, headings, and charts into writing
Week 31	REVIEW WEEK	**Informational Text:** Compare and contrast how different texts approach similar topics	Correctly identify and use past, present, and future verb tenses	**Informative:** Write a multi-paragraph essay with a clear structure and researched information
Week 32	Convert between different units of measurement within the same system	**Informational Text:** Use text features to locate information	Review grammar rules and language conventions	**Informative:** Peer edit and create a final writing draft

FIGURE 11.1 (Continued)

4th Grade

	Math	Reading	Language	Writing
Week 33	Solve real-world problems involving measurement in length, mass, and volume	**Informational Text:** Gather information from various texts to understand complex ideas	Review vocabulary learned throughout the year	**Opinion:** Research and gather facts to support an opinion
Week 34	Apply area and perimeter formulas to rectangles in real world problems	**Informational Text:** Revisit cause and effect relationships in informational texts	Apply what was learned with grammar and language conventions into writing	**Opinion:** Practice writing with a clear purpose and focus
Week 35	Draw points, lines, line segments, rays, and angles (right, acute, obtuse)	**Informational Text:** Evaluate the credibility and reliability of different informational sources	REVIEW WEEK	**Opinion:** Write a final draft with strong arguments, a clear introduction, and a conclusion
Week 36	Identify perpendicular and parallel lines as well as lines of symmetry	**Informational Text:** Deepen understanding of how an author's purpose influences the content of a text	REVIEW WEEK	**Opinion:** Peer edit and create a final draft

FIGURE 11.1 (Continued)

5th Grade

	Math	**Reading**	**Language**	**Writing**
Week 1	Understand place value for whole numbers and decimals to the thousandths place	**Literature:** Recognize story components like characters, setting, and plot	Review nouns, verbs, adjectives, adverbs, and prepositions	**Narrative:** Introduce narrative elements like characters, setting, and event sequences
Week 2	Round decimals to any place	**Literature:** Identify the theme of a story, and understand how it is conveyed through details	Understand simple, compound, and complex sentences	**Narrative:** Focus on developing characters and describing a setting
Week 3	Add and subtract decimals to the hundredths place	**Literature:** Compare and contrast characters, settings, or events in a story	The difference between using commas, parenthesis, and dashes	**Narrative:** Focus on transition words when managing event sequences
Week 4	Multiply whole numbers using the standard algorithm	**Literature:** Analyze the narrator's or speaker's point of view in a story	Use capitalization in various forms correctly	**Narrative:** Peer edit and revise. Write a final narrative draft
Week 5	Divide whole numbers with up to four-digit dividends and up to two-digit divisors using the standard algorithm	**Literature:** Identify and interpret figurative language in literature, like similes and metaphors	Form and use verb tenses appropriately	**Informative:** Introduce the structure of informative writing with an introduction, body, and conclusion
Week 6	Multiply decimals to the hundredths place	**Literature:** Explain how the structure of a story influences its meaning	Identify and use coordinating and subordinating conjunctions	**Informative:** Conduct research and organize relevant information
Week 7	Divide decimals to the hundredths place	**Literature:** Summarize stories focusing on key details and main ideas	Use commas after introductory elements, such as prepositional phrases	**Informative:** Write a draft that includes facts, details, and examples
Week 8	REVIEW WEEK	**Literature:** Compare and contrast themes across different stories	Identify and use prepositional phrases in writing	**Informative:** Peer edit, revise, and complete a final draft

FIGURE 11.1 (Continued)

5th Grade

	Math	Reading	Language	Writing
Week 9	Add fractions with unlike denominators	**Literature:** Summarize stories to determine their theme	Demonstrate understanding of synonyms and antonyms	**Opinion:** Introduce an opinion essay structure with an opinion, reasons, evidence, and a conclusion
Week 10	Subtract fractions with unlike denominators	**Informational Text:** Identify the main idea of a text and use key details to support it	Use quotation marks to indicate dialogue and direct quotes	**Opinion:** Practice linking opinions with logical reasons and supporting evidence
Week 11	Solve word problems involving adding and subtracting of fractions	**Informational Text:** Summarize the text using main ideas and key details	Correctly form and use comparative and superlative adjectives	**Opinion:** Write a complete opinion piece
Week 12	Multiply a fraction or whole number by a fraction	**Informational Text:** Analyze different text structures by using cause and effect	Use correct pronouns	**Opinion:** Peer edit, revise, and complete a final draft
Week 13	Solve word problems that involve multiplying fractions	**Informational Text:** Explore how text features like headings, captions, and diagrams help in locating information	Use commas to separate items in a series	**Narrative:** Focus on creating problems, rising action, and solutions within the narrative
Week 14	Divide fractions by whole numbers, and whole numbers by fractions	**Informational Text:** Use context clues to determine the meaning of unknown words and phrases	Understand and use similes and metaphors	**Narrative:** Create compelling introductions that hook a reader
Week 15	Solve word problems involving division of word problems	**Informational Text:** Analyze the author's purpose and how it influences the text	recognize and explain the meaning of common idioms and proverbs	**Narrative:** Focus on writing conclusions and resolving a story
Week 16	Practice multiplying and dividing fractions	**Informational Text:** Compare and contrast information from two or more texts on the same topic	Use context to determine the meaning of unknown words	**Narrative:** Peer edit, revise, and complete a final draft

FIGURE 11.1 (Continued)

5th Grade

	Math	Reading	Language	Writing
Week 17	REVIEW WEEK	**Informational Text:** Identify cause and effect in text	Identify and understand common Greek roots	**Informative:** Create multi-paragraph essays with clear organization
Week 18	Understand volume as an attribute of solid figures	**Informational Text:** Gather information from different sources to develop a comprehensive understanding	Identify and understand common Latin roots	**Informative:** Practice using important facts, definitions, and examples to explain ideas
Week 19	Measure volume using unit cubes	**Literature:** Revisit story elements and analyze how they work together to form a story	Use root words to expand vocabulary	**Informative:** Use text features like headings, diagrams, and charts to clarify information
Week 20	Calculate the volume of rectangular prisms	**Literature:** Explain how characters grow and change throughout a story	Use prefixes to determine word meanings	**Informative:** Peer edit, revise, and complete a finished draft
Week 21	Use the formula V = L x W x H to solve real-world problems	**Literature:** Explore how different narrators' points of view affect storytelling	Use suffixes to determine word meanings	**Opinion:** Introduce students to counterarguments and using them in their writing
Week 22	Plot points on the coordinate plan	**Literature:** Explain how figurative language contributes to the tone of a story	Review Greek and Latin Roots	**Opinion:** Use specific reasons and examples to support opinions
Week 23	Find the distance between two points on the coordinate plane	**Literature:** Compare and contrast two genres and their themes	Distinguish the meaning between different homophones	**Opinion:** Practice conclusions ending with a solid reasoning and restating an opinion
Week 24	Solve real-world problems using the coordinate plane	**Literature:** Analyze symbolism and how it conveys meaning in stories	Practice varying sentence length and structure	**Opinion:** Peer edit, revise, and write a final draft

FIGURE 11.1   (Continued)

5th Grade

	Math	**Reading**	**Language**	**Writing**
Week 25	Generate numerical patterns using given rules	**Literature:** Make inferences and draw conclusions from a story	Correctly form and use comparative and superlative adverbs	**Narrative:** Focus on developing characters through dialogue
Week 26	Form ordered pairs from patterns and graph the ordered pairs on the coordinate plane	**Literature:** Summarize stories using key details	Review correct usage of end punctuation	**Narrative:** Use figurative language to enhance descriptions in stories
Week 27	Attributes of 2D figures	**Literature:** Analyze dialogue and how it contributes to character development and plot	Expand vocabulary through word analysis and context	**Narrative:** Build suspense and engaging conflict in a plot
Week 28	Classify 2D figures in a hierarchy based on properties	**Informational Text:** Identify main ideas and key details while summarizes the text	Review figurative language including personification and hyperbole	**Narrative:** Peer edit, revise, and complete a final draft
Week 29	REVIEW WEEK	**Informational Text:** Use context clues to identify and understand vocabulary and phrases	Review pronouns, focusing on possessive pronouns	**Informative:** Focus on clear topic sentences and supporting details
Week 30	Interpret and create line plots to display data	**Informational Text:** Use multiple print and digital sources to gather information on a topic	Introduce colons and semicolons	**Informative:** Incorporate headings and charts into essays
Week 31	Solve problems using data from a line plot	**Informational Text:** Distinguish between primary and secondary sources and their roles in understanding a topic	Understand and use active and passive voice	**Informative:** Draft well-organized essay with facts and researched information
Week 32	Use parentheses, brackets, and/or braces in numerical expressions	**Informational Text:** Analyze bias and perspective in a text	Identify subtle differences and shades of meaning between words	**Informative:** Peer edit, revise and complete a final draft

FIGURE 11.1　(Continued)

5th Grade

	Math	Reading	Language	Writing
Week 33	Write and solve simple numerical expressions	**Informational Text:** Explore how cause and effect are presented in informational text	Vary sentences to improve writing	**Opinion:** Gather relevant facts to support opinions
Week 34	Convert between different sized units within the customary measurement system	**Informational Text:** Compare and contrast information from two or more texts on the same topic	Compare and contrast the varieties of English used in formal and informal language	**Opinion:** Maintain a clear focus throughout the opinion piece
Week 35	Convert between different sized units within the metric measurement system	**Informational Text:** Gather information from different texts to form an understanding on a topic	REVIEW WEEK	**Opinion:** Write a draft with strong arguments and clear structure
Week 36	REVIEW WEEK	**Informational Text:** Practice summarizing complex texts	REVIEW WEEK	**Opinion:** Peer edit, revise and complete a final draft

FIGURE 11.1 (Continued)

Get your free editable digital teacher planner template included with this book! Simply scan this QR code or type the link in your browser to get the bonus material.

teresakwant.com/bonus-material/
Password: levelup

CHAPTER 12

Bonus Level: Turn Your Passion into Profit

Sometimes, taking risks can be scary, especially if it's work you are putting out into the world that will be judged. During the beginning of my fourth year of teaching, I found an outlet where I could sell teaching materials online. I was just hoping to make a little bit of extra money to pay the grocery bill. Honestly, I doubted anyone would even want my lessons, and the thought of sharing my creations felt daunting. I wondered if what I was making was useful or if other teachers even needed the resources.

Despite my hesitations, I pushed forward. I decided to create a product to sell. I began with science materials because this was a subject that was challenging for me to teach. While math and language arts came naturally, science required extra effort on my part. I figured if science was difficult for me and if I couldn't find a lot of resources online to help me with my lessons, then other teachers just might find my resources helpful, too. It was this struggle that inspired my first product: a Moon Phases Folding Book.

It felt like a complete miracle. The day after posting my Moon Phases Folding Book on an online marketplace, I made a sale! I earned 30 cents, but it was the most impactful 30 cents of my life. In fact, it changed the trajectory of my career. That small sale showed me that a single lesson could have more value than I could ever imagine.

From there, I started creating writing units and literacy centers for upper elementary students. These were resources I needed in my own classroom. Along the way, I realized I had a lot to learn about becoming a business owner. For instance, I needed to find my true passion as a teacher-author and creator. Spoiler alert: It wasn't science! Yet, that single sale, the one small spark that started it all, was enough to open my eyes to the potential impact I could make beyond the four walls of my own classroom. That first sale was the first step that changed my life forever.

Soon, the extra income I was making from selling resources online was enough to cover more than just my grocery bills. Over time, after zeroing in on my niche and audience, I found a passion and direction that worked for me. Eventually, I worked my way to selling enough resources to far surpass my teaching income and started to bring in six figures annually with my business.

There are a few takeaways for why I believe my business was and is successful today. I would like to share those takeaways with you and give you some suggestions on how to start your own journey creating and selling resources. Whether you want to start a little side hustle so you can pay some extra bills, go on vacation, or just buy something new for yourself without worrying, let me give you some suggestions. You already have the keys necessary to create lesson plans that are leveled up and stand out, let's now get to the basics of how to take those ideas up a notch. Turning your passion into profit!

STEP 1: FIND YOUR PASSION AND NARROW YOUR NICHE

Your niche is the foundation for everything you create. So, when I say you should be passionate about it, I mean it! For instance, science was not my favorite subject to teach, but I found a hole in the market, and when I first started creating resources there weren't a lot of science materials for teachers on online marketplaces. My business brain was on the right track, but it was off just a little bit! It was great I found a problem to solve, but it was not a problem I *wanted* to undertake. Science was not my strong suit. In time, I would be burned out and exhausted and would not want to continue.

Eventually, I stumbled upon escape rooms and blending fun and gamification into the classroom while still sticking to educational standards and objectives. I created these resources with a math and language arts focus. It was important to find a niche I was passionate about, so even when I got overwhelmed or felt overworked, I wouldn't become burned out because I still loved my product.

Before you begin selling resources on an online marketplace, take some time to explore what excites you in your teaching practice. Maybe you love helping students find their creativity through art, encouraging explorations in STEAM, helping students develop social-emotional skills, or something else! Once you find that sweet spot—something you're passionate about and that fills a need for other teachers—you'll be ready to start building resources that not only benefit others but are fulfilling for you to create.

STEP 2: RESEARCH YOUR AUDIENCE'S NEEDS

Once you've nailed down your niche, the next essential step is understanding the unique needs of your audience. By identifying gaps in the market, you can provide resources that are valuable, practical, and unlike anything else out there. Being unique is key to finding success! Here are some strategies to help you pinpoint exactly what teachers in your audience need:

- **Start with your own classroom needs**: Think about what you need but can't easily find resources for. Often, your classroom insights reveal what's missing in the market. For example, one of my best-selling products came from a resource I couldn't find but desperately needed: I wanted literacy centers for upper elementary grades. At the time, this was very hard to find. So, I created them myself. Designing what you wish existed gives your resources authenticity and purpose.
- **Directly ask your audience**: One of the best ways to understand your audience's needs is to ask! Reach out to colleagues, friends, or teachers in online groups. If you have even a small social media following, use tools like polls or surveys to gather feedback. Each response offers valuable insight. Either it will point you in the right direction or it will help you weed out ideas that may not be relevant.

Knowing what your audience's challenges are makes a significant difference in the quality of your resources.

- **Stay informed on educational trends and standards**: Keeping up with current educational trends, curriculum shifts, and changes in standards helps you stay ahead of the market. For example, if there's an increased focus on social-emotional learning, you could create resources around this topic. This awareness keeps your resources relevant and in tune with teachers' evolving needs.

- **Tackle the "hard to create" resources**: Don't shy away from creating resources that seem complex or labor-intensive. In fact, run toward them! These "hard to create" materials often have less competition, making teachers more likely to buy a high-quality solution rather than attempting to make it themselves. When you create what others hesitate to, you position your resources as essential and high-value tools that teachers will return again and again for.

STEP 3: DESIGN QUALITY RESOURCES

To succeed as a seller, this is a step you simply can't overlook. Quality over quantity is essential to building a thriving business. Crafting a high-quality resource involves many elements, and truthfully, it's too much to cover in a single chapter! However, here's the good news: With your purchase of this book, you've received a *free* two-week trial in my Teacher-Author Brilliance Club. In the club, I guide you through each step, from product creation to launching your own business selling educational materials and everything in between.

To access your free two-week trial, simply scan this QR code.

teresakwant.com/bonus-material/
Password: levelup

I won't leave you hanging though. Let's dive into four foundational steps to help you create and prepare a resource that's ready to sell.

1. Decide what you want to create. This might take some research and time to plan. You might get going and your direction changes part way through. That's okay! My biggest suggestion is to *just start*. You can't go anywhere if you don't move. One of the hardest parts about deciding to start selling resources you create is actually getting started. If you are struggling with what to create, I suggest creating something that is seasonal. Maybe you want to create a back-to-school bulletin board kit or holiday-themed games. Whatever it is, get to work!

   Figure 12.1 shows a handy calendar that will outline popular themes and topics for each month of the year that appeal to teachers.

2. Once you have decided what to create, it is time to outline the resource! What standards will your resource focus on? What is the theme? What grade level(s) is it appropriate for? Will there be visuals? Should you include both a printable and digital resource? There are a lot of questions to ask yourself, so use the simple project template in Figure 12.2 to get started.

3. Now the fun begins! Choose a program to create your project in. The most accessible and easiest programs to use are either PowerPoint, Google Slides, or Canva. Each program has its own pros and cons for using it. My current favorites are PowerPoint and Canva. Just keep in mind that each program has its own set of terms of use, so you will need to make sure you follow the terms for commercially sold products.

4. Once your product is created, you will make a cover and preview for it. These pieces are important because they are the first things potential buyers see. They set the tone for how your resource is perceived. A professional and visually appealing cover can instantly grab the attention of a buyer and create a sense of trust and credibility. An eye-catching cover can communicate your product's key benefits quickly. A strong cover can also showcase your unique brand and style, helping you stand out in a crowded marketplace.

January	February
• New Year's Eve • New Year's Day • Goal Setting • Inauguration Day • Winter • Snow • Snowmen • Martin Luther King Day • 100th Day of School	• Black History Month • Groundhog Day • Valentine's Day • President's Day • Lunar New Year • Love • Hearts • Dental Health Month • Kindness
March	**April**
• Women's History Month • Spring • March Madness • Pi Day • St. Patrick's Day • Easter • Life Cycles • Weather • Reading	• Easter • Earth Day • Poetry Month • April Fool's Day • Spring • Library Week • Bunnies • Flowers • Insects
May	**June**
• Cinco De Mayo • Teacher Appreciation Week • Mother's Day • Memorial Day • End of the School Year • Summer • Graduation • Camping • Gardens	• Flag Day • Father's Day • Juneteenth • Summer • Ocean • Beach • Ice Cream • Fishing

FIGURE 12.1 Themes calendar

July	August
• Independence Day • America • Travel/Vacation • Hiking • Summer	• Back to School • Classroom Decor • Parent Forms • Meet the Teacher • All About Me • Watermelons • Friendships
September	**October**
• Back to School • Labor Day • Constitution Day • Hispanic Heritage Month • Fall • The Four Seasons • Apples • Johnny Apple Seed	• Fire Prevention Week • Halloween • Diwali • Pumpkins • Nocturnal Animals • Scarecrows • Bats • Fall • Spiders
November	**December**
• National American Indian Heritage Month • Veteran's Day • Election Day • Thanksgiving • Harvest • Families • Hibernation • Leaves	• Christmas • Hanukkah • Kwanzaa • Winter • Snow • Gingerbread • Candy Canes • Christmas Around the World • Holidays Around the World

FIGURE 12.1 (Continued)

Project Outline Planner

Project Name:	Due Date:

Tools and Resources Needed:	Notes:

Tasks and Deadlines

Task	Start Date	Deadline

End Objective:

FIGURE 12.2 Project outline planner

The preview is equally important because it gives buyers an inside look at your product, allowing them to feel confident in their purchase. A well-organized preview that highlights essential pages or features can answer questions before they are asked because buyers want to know what is inside and what they are purchasing. Buyers want resources that are well-structured, easy to use, and classroom ready. By offering a sneak peek into the quality of your resource, you're providing reassurance that your product solves a teacher's problem instantly.

STEP 4: CREATING TITLES AND DESCRIPTIONS

Creating strong titles and descriptions for your products on their marketplace is essential for success because they play a major role in attracting potential buyers. A well-written title and description makes your product easy to find. Using relevant keywords that teachers are likely to search for helps the product stand out, too. The title should give your buyers an immediate understanding about what your product is, whom it is for, and what problem it solves. By using specific terms that resonate with your target audience, like grade level, subject, and unique features, you improve the chances of your product appearing in search results for the teachers you want to see your product.

The product description is equally important because it gives a teacher a clear, detailed understanding of not only your product's content but its purpose in the classroom and the benefits it offers to the teacher. A strong description highlights how the resource will save teachers time, engage students, and meet specific standards, therefore giving the teacher a compelling reason to purchase the product. A good description answers the most pressing questions a customer may ask about your product and reduces hesitation in why it is needed. Additionally, a good description helps set realistic expectations, minimizing dissatisfaction from customers.

STEP 5: PRICING TIPS

There are lots of factors when determining how to price your product for sale. While offering products for free can be a strategy, it's best to reserve this for smaller items or samples of larger products. Don't underestimate your value and the impact of what you've created! Imposter syndrome is real and might begin to creep in. Push it away, quickly! What you have to share with the world is important, unique, and needed. If your resource is valuable to you, trust that it will be valuable to other teachers as well.

There are different methods when approaching pricing products. Items teachers consider when pricing a resource might include pages in the resource, value, digital components, time, and effort required to make the product, or similar products on the market. I suggest starting by looking at the page length of your product first. A general guideline would be to start with $0.10–$0.25 per page. However, take into account if you are creating basic worksheets with fill-in-the-blank questions, a product with similar pages that are copy and pasted (like flashcards), or detailed pages with reading passages that take research to write. A more comprehensive product could justify a higher per-page rate.

I recommend starting with a per-page pricing approach, but don't rely solely on this method; there are several other important factors to consider as well. For example, you may research other similar products in your niche or grade level. Analyze their pricing structure, and decide on a price that is competitive for what is out in the market already, in regard to what you've created. You may even consider pricing your resource slightly lower than other sellers and, as you earn positive reviews, gradually increasing your price. Don't forget your expertise and time and effort investing into each product. A more complex product, with unique elements, typically can justify a higher pricing. Multiday lessons, bundles, or resources with differentiated levels, answer keys, or editable versions can also justify higher prices as opposed to a single-use product with simpler materials.

Other pricing strategies might include pricing resources at prices like $4.99 instead of $5.00. There is psychology in pricing, and people prefer to see the 4 instead of the 5. You may also consider offering sales with your products when released. I like to offer products 50 percent off for the first 24 hours they are released. This offers urgency and makes return customers of my buyers. They follow my store and watch for my sales so they can grab the resources at discounts when released.

STEP 6: PRODUCT LINES AND BUNDLING

Creating product lines and bundling options is a powerful way to enhance your store's value and establish your brand identity. While this strategy is closely related to pricing as well, it deserves its own focus because it involves more than just setting prices: It's about building a cohesive brand, products that stand out and attracting loyal buyers as you meet their evolving needs. With well-thought-out product lines and bundles, you can offer teachers an all-in-one solution, making your resources more appealing and convenient while potentially increasing your sales, too.

Developing a product line allows you to organize your resources into cohesive, themed categories, making it easy for buyers to find related items and understand the focus of your store. For example, if you specialize in reading comprehension resources, you might create product lines based on grade levels, genres, or specific skills, such as "Third-Grade Reading Passages" or " Inference Practice Units." As teachers start to recognize the consistency and quality of each product line, they're more likely to return to your store for related resources.

A well-organized series of product lines also increases your store's visibility on online marketplaces. When teachers find a resource they love in one product line, they're more likely to explore other items within the same category. This keeps your buyers engaged with your store and builds brand loyalty. Teachers will associate your store with reliable, comprehensive resources. Over time, you can create brand consistency, which will help you build a loyal customer base of returning teachers who leave positive reviews and share about your store.

Bundling is an effective way to offer value to buyers while increasing your sales. When you bundle products that naturally complement each other—such as seasonal activities, unit lesson plans, or resources that follow a skill progression—teachers benefit by getting everything they need in one purchase, often at a slightly reduced rate compared to buying each product separately. The built-in discount that is felt with bundles encourages teachers to purchase the bundle because it is a better value. Bundles may also improve customer satisfaction because you gave them a complete solution, making it easier for them to implement consistency in their classroom.

Let's not just glaze over the benefit of discounting bundles. Teachers feel they're getting more value for their money, which can make them more likely to purchase the bundle over the individual item. Consider a bundle discount of 10–20 percent so as to provide value but not cut into your own earnings. Promoting bundles during key seasons, like back-to-school season or Black Friday and Cyber Monday, can drive more traffic to your store and business, providing interest in your resources.

By creating product lines and bundling complementary resources, you're not only building a more organized and professional store but also offering added value to your customers. This approach sets you apart from other sellers as teachers recognize your commitment to quality, consistency, and convenience. With time, product lines and bundles can become the cornerstone of your brand, attracting repeat buyers and solidifying your store's place in the marketplace. I highly suggest when creating products that you keep in mind product lines, eventually bundling products together.

WRAPPING IT UP

Entering the world of online marketplaces for teacher resources is an exciting journey that offers the opportunity to share your expertise and passion with other educators and ideally in the process allow you to earn a little extra cash in your pocket. While starting might seem daunting, focusing on high-quality, classroom-tested products, crafting engaging covers and previews, setting thoughtful pricing, and building a brand through product lines and bundling can set you on a path to success. Each element contributes to building trust, attracting loyal customers, and ultimately growing a sustainable business that benefits both you and the teachers who use your resources.

Every teacher who sells products will have a unique journey. There's no single "right" way to grow your business. Don't be afraid to experiment with different strategies, learn from your successes and setbacks, and continue to refine your approach. This is a learning experience, and as time goes on, you will get better and better at the process. As you gain confidence and see the impact your resources have on other classrooms. You'll find joy not only in additional income but also in knowing that your hard work is making a difference in education.

Above all, stay committed to your passion for teaching and learning. As you build your online presence and reach more educators, let your purpose guide you, creating resources that inspire, support, and empower teachers everywhere. With patience and dedication, you'll create a thriving teacher business that continues to grow and evolve, helping you reach your goals while making a meaningful impact in classrooms around the world.

CONCLUSION

A memory that will always stay with me is the day I made the difficult decision to step away from my role as a classroom teacher to focus on raising my children. I realize this is not a privilege everyone can make, and I am humbled I could take this opportunity; however, that doesn't negate the fact that, emotionally, it was a very difficult decision. I still remember the overwhelming panic I felt after telling my principal that I would not be returning the following year. On the drive home, I experienced a full-blown panic attack, and my chest tightened, my breath felt shallow, and tears streamed down my face. I had to pull over, roll down my windows, and take a moment to gather myself before finishing the drive home. It was one of the most emotionally uncertain times in my life. I kept asking myself if I was making the right choice.

Teaching has always been my ultimate goal. I had reached that dream and was thriving as a sixth-grade teacher. I loved the work and found immense fulfillment in helping my students grow and succeed. But as life evolved and I started a family, my priorities began to shift. Balancing the demands of being both a teacher and a full-time mom proved unsustainable for me personally. To those of you who manage to wear both badges—teacher and parent—I hold the deepest respect for you. It is a role that requires endless strength and resilience, and it is by no means for the faint of heart.

As I moved forward in my professional journey, I learned something profound even if clichéd: once you're a teacher, you're always a teacher. Although my classroom looks different now, I still live the role every day, whether I'm helping teachers build successful side hustles or guiding educators how to incorporate technology like Canva into their lesson planning, the title of teacher remains a core part of who I am. It's not just a job; it's an identity that shapes everything I do, and that will never change.

As educators, you have the incredible responsibility and privilege of shaping the minds of future generations. Throughout this book, we've explored creative ways to bring joy, engagement, learning, and innovation into the classroom. From simple engaging hooks to collaborative escape rooms that capture the imaginations of your students, together we've unlocked a treasure trove of tools that can transform ordinary lessons into extraordinary learning experiences.

By leveling up your lesson plans, you are not only meeting your students where they are but also inspiring them to think critically, collaborate effectively, and approach challenges with curiosity. You've been equipped with strategies to adapt to diverse learning needs, incorporate technology, and bring collaboration to the center of your lessons. The journey doesn't need to end here! Every lesson, set of students, and new school year brings an opportunity to try something new, reflect on what works, and refine your approach to teaching.

As you begin to move forward, I encourage you to embrace the spirit of creativity and collaboration that we've discussed. Challenge yourself to find new ways to engage your students and cultivate a love for learning. The possibilities are endless, and your students will thrive in an environment that is both fun and educational. So, teacher friend, it's time to press play, level up, and continue the quest to make learning an exciting and enriching experience. Your journey is just beginning: game on!

About the Author

Teresa Kwant is an educator, curriculum designer, and business mentor with more than 12 years of experience creating engaging resources for teachers and students. A former elementary school teacher with a technology endorsement and a graduate of the University of Utah, Teresa combines classroom expertise with innovation to craft high-quality educational materials. Her mission is to make learning engaging and interactive, through game-based learning, technology, and collaborative activities.

As a platinum seller on Teachers Pay Teachers (TPT), Teresa's resources have reached classrooms worldwide, empowering teachers with practical and engaging tools. She is a sought-after speaker at TPT Forward conferences and virtual summits, where she shares strategies for integrating technology and design into teaching. Her courses and live trainings help educators and aspiring entrepreneurs build successful businesses and bring creativity to their classrooms.

Teresa lives in Salt Lake City, Utah, with her husband and three children, balancing family life with her career as a curriculum designer in the education community. Her dedication to innovation and teaching continues to make a lasting impact on educators and students alike. Visit https://teresakwant.com to learn more about Teresa's work and to access inspiring ideas for educators.

Index